| Vote required? | Applies to what motions? | Motions can have what applied to it (in addition to withdraw)? | Can be renewed? |
| --- | --- | --- | --- |
| majority | no other motion | no other motion | yes[2] |
| majority | no other motion | amend[1] | yes[2] |
| no vote | no other motion | no other motion | yes[2] |
| majority | main, amend, appeal | no other motion | yes[2] |
| two-thirds | debatable motions | no other motion | yes[2] |
| two-thirds | debatable motions | amend[1] | yes[2] |
| majority | main motion | amend,[1] vote immediately, limit debate | yes[2] |
| majority | main, amend | vote immediately, limit debate | yes[2] |
| majority | variable in form | subsidiary motions, reconsider | no |
| majority | main motion | vote immediately, limit debate | no |
| majority | no motion | specific main, subsidiary, object to consideration | no |
| majority | main, amend, appeal | vote immediately, limit debate, postpone definitely | no |
| majority | main motion | all subsidiary motions | no |
| majority | main, amend, appeal | no other motion | yes[2] |
| majority | main motion | amend | yes[2] |
| tie or majority | decisions of chair | reconsider, limit debate, vote immediately, postpone temporarily or definitely | no |
| no vote | any error | no other motion | no |
| no vote | no motion | no other motion | no |
| no vote | all motions | none | yes[2] |
| two-thirds | no mot... | | no |
| two-thirds neg. | main m... | | yes[2] |
| no vote | main, a... | | no |
| no vote | voice vo... | | no |

...parliamentary situation.

# ADVISORY COMMITTEE

*Sturgis* STANDARD CODE OF

# PARLIAMENTARY PROCEDURE

*Sturgis* STANDARD CODE OF

# PARLIAMENTARY PROCEDURE

❖ ❖ ❖ ❖ ❖ ❖ ❖

*by Alice F. Sturgis*

*McGraw-Hill Book Company, Inc.*
*New York     London     Toronto*

STURGIS STANDARD CODE OF PARLIAMENTARY
PROCEDURE

Published by the McGraw-Hill Book Company, Inc.
Printed in the United States of America

# PREFACE

When Winston Churchill, during the abdication crisis in 1936, rose before a shocked House of Commons to answer Mr. Baldwin's statement and to discuss the constitutional question before a final decision was made, the House was in a hostile temper. A burst of disapproval greeted the great statesman. Churchill set his pugnacious jaw and, as the uproar subsided, declared:

"If the House resists my claim [to speak] it will only add more importance to any words that I may use."

Here in the mother of parliaments, which has lent its name to the system of rules by which assemblies are conducted, we see at work the fundamental principles of democratic discussion. Here was the right of free and fair debate, the right of the majority to decide, and the right of the minority to protest and to be protected. Here also was a demonstration that the violation of rights in public assemblies lends weight to the cause of the suppressed. The majority may rule, but it must rule fairly and wisely. Its rule must be validated by respect for those who oppose it. In turn, the minority, once the vote has been taken, has the duty of accepting the decision and abiding by the general mandate.

Here is the essence of the democratic procedure of free assemblies, whether they be the House of Commons, the United States Congress, or a high-school debating society— a procedure based on what Jefferson called "equal and exact justice to all men."

Modern man lives in a multitude of groups: civic, labor, trade and business, religious, fraternal, academic, and cultural. Men join organizations because they agree with their avowed purposes; they form new ones in order to achieve certain aims. But as soon as men combine one with another they must have rules to guide and control their actions. There must be rules and procedures in order to conduct discussion, to effect action, to resolve conflicts, and, indeed, in order to work together at all.

The purpose of parliamentary law is to assist an assembly in carrying out its purposes. It is the code of ethics of working together—the rules of the game. Parliamentary law is concerned with the means by which beliefs and ideas are best translated into effective group action. It must provide orderly ways of determining the will of the majority. It must be clear, considerate, kind, fair, and it must effect the desired aims of the assembly. It must, in other words, be democratic.

There is nothing the world of today needs more urgently than men and women who have the fundamental skill of working together. That skill, and the desire to work together democratically, can be augmented by a parliamentary code based on invariable principles, common procedures in actual use, and on the large number of court decisions that have been rendered in the past three-quarters of a century. The present work is intended to fulfill these needs.

In preparing this new standard code the author has tried to make it conform to seven basic principles which would make the code completely usable and modern:

1. *Completeness.* All sources of parliamentary law were checked, all rules were diagramed and catalogued, to be certain that every essential point had been included. On the other hand, many suppositions and arbitrary rules that have not proved workable and practical were eliminated.

2. *Simplicity and Clarity.* Every effort has been made to achieve simplicity and clarity. This code has been planned for easy reference and for adoption as a guide. It may be used by educational and professional societies, religious bodies, trade associations and labor unions, commercial and civic organizations, schools, clubs, and veterans' organizations. Since it covers the whole field of parliamentary procedure, it should fulfill all of their needs. The author has made a special effort to dispel ambiguity and has discarded misleading terms, which serve only to befuddle the uninitiated, in favor of self-explanatory ones.

The basic parliamentary rules are explained so that one may reason out the answers and thus eliminate the necessity for memorizing hundreds of technical rules. Given a clear understanding of fundamental concepts, most of the rules governing them become self-evident.

3. *Conciseness.* Clarity solves only half the problems of a good code. No one book, however voluminous, can answer every detail of every situation. On the other hand, if one understands the fundamental principles upon which procedure is based, he can usually deduce the correct rules. Just as the law lays down the general principles to be followed, and the judge decides how a particular principle applies to a specified set of facts, so the presiding officer is the judge in deliberative societies. The general rules of parliamentary procedure are his guide.

4. *Usability.* Each motion is discussed under uniform headings, which makes reference to any desired fact simple and easy. The purpose of the motion, its form, an explana-

tion of its characteristics, its effect, and the rules governing
it are set forth completely, separately, clearly, and for the
first time in this fashion. Answers to many fundamental
questions can be found quickly and easily by reference to
tables and lists. Hundreds of minor rules have been distilled
into a few general rules.

5. *Common Procedures*. Every rule in this book has been
proved by experience, tested by practice, and has the pres-
tige of general acceptance. Special attention has been given
to common procedures in actual use. The author has drawn
on years of observation and experience, and on thousands of
interviews with many large national organizations, including
such diverse groups as the most powerful trade unions and
the United States Chamber of Commerce. The purpose of
this research was to find out what successful organizations
are doing and how these things could be done better. This
method elicited the contribution of many ideas and suggestions. It revealed trends and tendencies and disclosed out-
moded rules.

6. *Conformance to Court Decisions*. For the first time, a
work on parliamentary law has been closely integrated with
court decisions. This omission in the past has led many
organizations into expensive and troublesome litigation. It
is important that groups and the members of groups know
their rights and obligations. Questions arising out of parliamentary law have appeared in the courts for adjudication
since Colonial times but have been overlooked or ignored
by parliamentary writers. In the preparation of this code
approximately 3000 court cases were considered. All rules are
stated in conformity to these decisions and to the laws governing organizations. Hundreds of lawsuits could have been
avoided had there been available to organizations a code
which was correct both from a parliamentary and a legal
standpoint.

7. *Up-to-dateness.* Care has been taken to explain the advantages of modern practices. For example, special emphasis has been placed on the importance of helping committees to function effectively. Timesaving methods to be used in meetings and conventions are explained, and many efficient shortcuts are suggested.

In this volume are stated and discussed fundamental principles which provide basic understanding of parliamentary procedure. During centuries of usage, parliamentary law has grown into a body of established rules. It is a collection of principles based on the rule of the majority, a principle that flourishes in democratic countries. At the same time it must live and change. No one will deny that our procedure should evolve, grow, and serve faithfully the purposes of free societies. No one has expressed better the evolutionary character of parliamentary law than Thomas Jefferson, who wrote in the preface of his manual:

"I have begun a sketch, which those who come after me will successively correct and fill up, till a code of rules shall be formed . . . the effects of which may be accuracy in business, economy of time, order, uniformity and impartiality."

These principles have guided us in the preparation of this code.

*Alice F. Sturgis*

# ACKNOWLEDGMENTS

This book is the fulfillment of a project in which many outstanding persons have had a part.

It draws its strength and completeness from the broad experience and sound judgment of leaders in many fields. From the inception of the project to the completion of this code these individuals have made vital contributions; some from a background of long experience and some from a special knowledge of a particular problem. To those who have helped in so many ways I express my deepest gratitude.

Harold H. Burton, Justice of the Supreme Court of the United States and author of the Foreword, has accurately and inspiringly expressed the relationship between parliamentary procedure and democracy. The code has also benefited by suggestions arising from his service as a senator of the United States and his experience as a justice of the Supreme Court.

Owen J. Roberts, an outstanding justice of the Supreme Court of the United States for fifteen years and now Dean of the School of Law at the University of Pennsylvania, wrote the forceful Introduction. His wide judicial experience and his achievements in the field of education lend unusual weight to his comments.

The text of the code from beginning to completion is stamped by the sound judgment and logical criticism of Paul Mason, authority on constitutional law, parliamentarian of broad experiences and author of *Mason's Manual of Legislative Procedure.*

The extensive research of Kenwood Sturgis on several important phases of the law in their relation to parliamentary procedure rates him also as a working co-author.

From the beginning of this project Professor James E. Brenner of the School of Law of Stanford University has given active help and practical encouragement. Also at Stanford University, Professor Leland Chapin has tested the details of the code while it was still in manuscript form by using it in his classes in the Graduate School of Business. Professor James Gordon Emerson of the School of Speech, who teaches pre-legal argumentation, read the manuscript and supplied detailed corrections.

Paul G. Hoffman, President of the Ford Foundation, was a most helpful godfather to the project. He made valuable suggestions which proved to be sound and wise.

Milton A. Smith, Assistant Counsel, Chamber of Commerce of the United States, gave extensive assistance and made a helpful survey through his organization on the current practices of committees.

Arthur W. Eckman, General Counsel, First Church of Christ, Scientist, offered expert parliamentary advice and support.

Martha Lee Carter, Parliamentarian of the Senior Congressional Club of Washington, D. C., interviewed leaders in Congress and successfully prodded those working on the project.

T. V. McDavitt, Counsel and Director, Bureau of Industrial and Personnel Relations, American Medical Association, was extremely helpful in pointing out present parliamentary trends.

In the South, Colonel Blake R. Van Leer, President of the Georgia Institute of Technology, offered constant encouragement and suggestions.

James A. Farley, former Postmaster General, drew on his vast experience to furnish practical material on conventions, while Olive H. Huston, Executive Secretary of the National Federation of the Business and Professional Women's Clubs, who makes conventions her hobby, also contributed excellent ideas.

Keith Seegmiller, General Counsel of the National Association of County Officials, furnished extensive material about county legislative bodies and their practices.

George H. Wilson, Director of the American Farm Bureau Federation, explained very effectively the interest of the many farm groups in parliamentary procedure and their experiences with its use.

Albert J. Harno, Dean of the College of Law at the University of Illinois, lent his support, understanding, and experience to the project.

The Honorable Clarence Cannon, author of *Cannon's Precedents,* pointed out decisively the difference between the parliamentary rules needed by highly specialized legislative bodies, such as Congress, and the established procedures of ordinary deliberative groups.

Fritz Roethlisberger, Associate Professor of Industrial Research of the Harvard Graduate School of Business Administration, was very helpful with material concerning the relation of the individual to groups and to parliamentary procedure.

John F. Malley, Chairman and Counsel of the Board of Trustees of the Elks National Foundation, gave helpful counsel from his long experience as a lawyer on how groups could avoid litigation by following correct procedure.

Douglas L. Edmonds, Associate Justice of the Supreme Court of California, aided with ideas for simplifying the language of parliamentary procedure to make it more useful to more people.

Phil S. Grant, Professor of English at the University of California, read the manuscript and supplied excellent criticism.

Melvin Jones, Secretary of the International Association of Lions Clubs, was generous with his time and suggestions.

Joseph Henry Jackson, author and literary critic, has been consistently helpful with technical advice on the manner of presenting material in the code.

Professor Donald Kirk David, Dean of the Graduate School of Business Administration of Harvard University, supplied material on the relationship of parliamentary procedure to business organizations with particular reference to committees and conferences.

Daniel L. Marsh, President of Boston University, has supplied information on parliamentary law as practiced by church groups from his long experience.

Arthur T. Vanderbilt, Chief Justice of the Supreme Court of New Jersey, was very cooperative and helpful in exploring the relationship of parliamentary procedure to the practice of law.

Reginald Heber Smith, Executive Secretary of the Commission for the Survey of the Legal Profession of the American Bar Association, helped to coordinate this project with the work of that committee.

Mark Starr, Educational Director of the International Ladies Garment Workers Union, made available his fine collection of parliamentary material prepared for labor unions.

Nellie Fleming, Parliamentarian of the General Federation of Women's Clubs and of the Daughters of the American Revolution, was most generous in discussing theories of parliamentary law growing out of her wide activities as a parliamentarian for women's organizations.

Charles Watkins, Parliamentarian of the Senate of the United States, discussed in detail his belief in the need for more complete differentiation between the parliamentary law used by Congress and by ordinary bodies.

Ruth Bottomly, Director of Office of the National Congress of Parents and Teachers, assisted with a discussion of the importance of maintaining continuity of policies in national organizations, and how such continuity might be maintained.

Colonel William A. Roberts, Counsel and Parliamentarian of the AMVETS, of Washington, D. C., an attorney with extensive background in setting up and operating organizations, contributed valuable material on organizing groups.

Robert H. Eckhoff and Eugene K. Sturgis of the California Bar served as ever-ready and interested consultants on difficult legal problems.

Many other leaders were kind enough to arrange rewarding interviews or to give other assistance. Among them were Thomas E. Dewey, Governor of New York State; Richard Chamberlain, former State Commander of the American Legion; Donald Blair Rice, past President of Kiwanis International; Philip Lovejoy, Secretary of Rotary International; Dr. Kathryn McHale, General Director of the American Association of University Women; Judge Orie Phillips, Chairman of the Council of the Survey of the Legal Profession; Matthew Woll, Counsel of the American Federation of Labor; Lowell Thomas, Commentator; Kathleen H. Rideout, Delta Delta Delta Sorority.

The Advisory Committee includes some of the most experienced leaders in organization work and some of the best minds of our time. Their worthy council and critical intelligence have been the cornerstone of this code. Their advice will guide its future.

ALICE F. STURGIS

# CONTENTS

# Part Two: ORGANIZATIONS—Their Structure and Functions

# Part Three: MOTIONS

# FOREWORD

Parliamentary law is applied not only by legislatures, executives, and courts but by many others. Parliamentary procedure is to legislation what court procedure is to litigation. It is essential to competent self-government. It also can help any group make up its mind. It leads, as promptly, fairly, and intelligently as possible, to the discovery of high common factors of agreement.

Free people will do well to learn its elements with their alphabets and use them in every policy-forming group—from a troop of Scouts to the Parliament of Man. It requires the wishes of a deliberative body to be ascertained with justice to each member, and when so ascertained, it expects each member to abide by them.

This book explains how diverse views in any group may be brought to an issue by orderly discussion and converted into majority action. Such procedure enables free people to take united action and yet retain the greatest individual freedom consistent with the interests of all. It is a precious passkey to peace and good will.

*Associate Justice*
*Supreme Court of the United States*

# INTRODUCTION

This volume will supply a real need. It is not a mere manual of procedure, a mere catalogue of rules and their precedence. On the contrary, it is a complete exposition of the fundamental concepts which underlie the rules. One who wishes to become a parliamentarian will find it unique, both in its statement of the philosophy on which the system is founded, and in its integration of specific rules under the principles which have evoked them.

The reader who masters the book will find himself a skilled parliamentarian, who knows not merely the appropriate rule, and its place in the hierarchy, but the reasons for the rule and for its order of precedence.

The style is clear and terse and the order of treatment logical. The material is presented in an interesting way, tending to attract and hold the attention of the reader, but there is no unnecessarily long explanation or discussion. A pioneer feature is the citation in notes of about one hundred and fifty court decisions supporting the principles stated in the text. It is surprising that so often parliamentary rulings have been the subject of adjudication by the courts. There is also a useful glossary and a table showing the precedence of the various appropriate motions.

No such complete book on parliamentary procedure has been produced. The work should take a commanding place in the field.

*Owen J. Roberts*

*Dean, The Law School, University*
*of Pennsylvania*
*Former Associate Justice of the*
*Supreme Court of the United States*

# PART I
## PROCEDURE—ITS PRINCIPLES AND
### GENERAL RULES

# Chapter 1. FUNDAMENTAL PRINCIPLES

## OF PARLIAMENTARY LAW

### Principles Determine Rules

A knowledge of the basic principles upon which parliamentary law rests enables one to reason out the answers to most parliamentary questions. A thorough understanding of these fundamental principles and their implications will clarify the whole subject of parliamentary procedure. Although there are only a few simple fundamental principles upon which parliamentary procedure is based, there are hundreds of rules which derive from these principles. If you learn the basic principles, it will be very easy to learn the rules because most of them follow logically from the principles. Also from these principles you can usually reason out the correct answers to numerous questions too detailed to be covered by specific rules.

The most important principles underlying parliamentary procedure are the following:

1. *Parliamentary rules exist to facilitate the transaction of business and to promote cooperation and harmony.* The philosophy of parliamentary law is constructive. It is designed

to facilitate and to help rather than to hinder or to obstruct. Parliamentary procedure is not to be used for dilatory purposes. Its aim is not to confuse, to mislead, or to thwart an honest expression of the majority's will.

It is not a technical device to be used to awe or entangle or confound the uninitiated. Overly technical use of rules to defeat the majority's will is a misuse of rules. Technical rules should be applied only to the extent necessary to expedite business, to avoid confusion, and to protect the rights of members.

2. *The vote of the majority decides.* The ultimate authority of an organization is vested in the majority of its members. This is a fundamental concept of democratic institutions. Freedom-loving peoples are not willing to be controlled by less than a majority.

Whenever more than a majority vote is required to take an action, the minority is given the power to defeat the will of the majority. Thus, if a three-fourths vote is required, the will of the group can be defeated by any number exceeding one-fourth of its members.

The main purpose of parliamentary procedure is to ascertain the will of the majority and to see that this will is carried out. When the will of the majority has been expressed by a vote, that vote becomes the decision of the organization. Once the vote has been announced, the minority has the duty to accept the decision and abide by the general mandate. Every member agrees tacitly, when he joins a group, to be governed by the vote of the majority.

3. *All members have equal rights, privileges, and obligations.* Equality is a basic democratic principle. Every member has an equal right or privilege to propose motions or bring up other business, to speak and to be protected from interruption, to ask questions, to nominate, and to vote. Particularly, each member has the right to insist on the strict

and impartial application of any rule necessary to protect him or any other member in his rights and privileges.

This equality of rights and privileges has a corollary of equality of duties and obligations. The presiding officer must see that this equitable balance of rights and obligations is maintained between members.

4. *The minority has rights which must be protected.* There are certain basic rights belonging to a minority which democratic institutions always protect. The decision belongs to the majority, but the right to discuss, the right to be heard, and the right to oppose are valued rights of a minority which should not be infringed upon.[1]

This protection of the rights of the minority should be the concern of every member. The minority of today is frequently the majority of tomorrow. A member of the majority on one question may be in the minority on the next question.

5. *Full and free discussion of every proposition presented for decision is an established right.* It is also a basic democratic concept. Each member of the assembly has the fundamental right to express his opinion fully and freely without interruption or interference so long as he remains within the rules of decorum. Motions which seek to curb or restrict this right, such as the motions to limit debate or to vote immediately (previous question), require a two-thirds vote because they supersede this fundamental right of full and free discussion. The right of every member to "have his say," "to have his day in court," or "to be heard" is as important as his right to vote.

6. *The simplest and most direct procedure for accomplishing a purpose should be followed.* This requirement is necessary to save time and effort and to avoid confusion. This principle prevents the use of parliamentary procedure to confuse by taking devious routes and multiplying technicalities.

A chairman should generally rule motions out of order if they present needless complications or when, as Thomas Jefferson said, "the same result may be be had more simply."

If a member undertakes a circuitous approach to a problem, the chairman should suggest the most direct and simplest procedure for accomplishing the purpose. For example, if a member proposes to amend a motion by striking out a word and proposes to follow this by another amendment to insert a different word in the same place, these two amendments should be combined into one amendment to substitute the latter word for the original word.

7. *Motions have a definite and logical order of precedence.* This precedence or priority is based on the relative urgency or necessity of each motion in relation to the efficient transaction of business.

It is this principle of orderly and definite precedence which prevents motions from piling up in confused entanglement. With each motion holding a fixed rank for its introduction and consideration, business can move ahead smoothly and swiftly.

To illustrate, if a main motion is being considered, a motion to amend is in order and takes precedence over the main motion. This is the proper sequence because it is necessary to correct or perfect the motion before it is voted upon.

8. *Every member has the right to know at all times what question is before the assembly and what its effect will be.* The presiding officer should keep the question to be voted upon clearly before the assembly and, when necessary, he should explain procedural motions and their effects before calling for a vote on them.

For example, if during the consideration of a motion some member says, "I move the previous question," members unskilled in parliamentary law are entitled to be informed that if this motion is adopted, debate will be cut off immediately.

This principle underlies the right of a member to request information or to rise to a parliamentary inquiry. It is a precept of parliamentary law that every action taken by a deliberative body should be taken intelligently.

9. *Only one question can be considered at a time.* In the interests of orderly procedure this principle is fundamental. When one motion is under consideration, it can be superseded by a motion having a higher precedence, which then becomes the motion under consideration. This latter motion can in turn be superseded, but each motion is considered separately and in turn so that only one question is before the assembly at one time.

There may be many parliamentary complications which arise from the one proposition before the assembly, but by following the fundamental rule of considering one question at a time, the assembly will find its way clearly through these complications.

10. *Those to whom power is delegated must be chosen by democratic processes.* Democracies operate, not by direct participation of every member in every process of democracy, but by the delegation of power to a few, who are chosen by a vote of the majority. Power is delegated to committees, to boards, to officers, and to representatives, but this delegation must be made directly or indirectly by the democratic process of a majority vote.

A self-appointed officer or a self-perpetuating board would violate the right of the members of an organization to delegate their power only to leaders chosen by their vote. The presiding officer is usually delegated the authority to appoint committees, but this is given by majority vote and can be controlled or withdrawn by a majority at any time. This principle of choice by democratic process underlies the usual provision in the bylaws that officers shall be elected by ballot.

11. *The presiding officer should be strictly impartial.* The presiding officer can best serve the interests of an organization by being strictly impartial toward members or groups of the organization. He should assist the organization in reaching its decisions and be guided by those decisions. He should not participate in controversies. He serves as the honored but impartial servant of the assembly.

The presiding officer should not be a partisan in debate. If there is information which the assembly needs, he may call upon some other member to present it. If no other member has the information, the presiding officer may present it from the chair. If the presiding officer considers that it is essential to argue any question, he has the right to do so, but this right should be used very sparingly. He leaves his position as presiding officer and calls upon the vice-chairman to preside while he speaks from the floor.

To preserve his impersonality, he always refers to himself as "the chair," "the chairman," or "the presiding officer."

## Importance of Basic Principles

At first reading, these basic principles may seem almost self-evident. Like the principles on which democracies are based, they are so simple and familiar that we sometimes fail to recognize their importance. Yet as basic democratic principles they serve as a foundation on which the framework of group procedure is built. Anyone who desires to understand the fundamentals by which people work successfully in groups will do well to read and reread these fundamental principles of parliamentary law.

## Chapter 2. ORDER OF BUSINESS

### Usual Order of Business

Most organizations have a bylaw which sets forth the order of business or the business program for each meeting. When the bylaws do not specify an order of business, the following order is followed:

1. Call to order
2. Reading or disposition of minutes of previous meeting
3. Reports of boards and standing committees
4. Reports of special committees
5. Unfinished business
6. New business
7. Announcements
8. Adjournment

When there is an invocation or prayer, it follows the call to order. If the roll of members is called, this precedes the reading of the minutes.

### Flexibility in the Order of Business

The purpose of an order of business is to secure a more orderly and expeditious conduct of business. While it should be adhered to in general, there should be a reasonable flexibility. The order of business should not be permitted to interfere with the business of a meeting. For example, if a special committee is ready to report but a standing committee is not yet ready, the presiding officer should not hesitate to call upon the chairman of the special committee to report. At a meeting of a board or committee considerable latitude in varying the order of business is essential.

The order of business of a convention should be prepared to fulfill the particular needs of the convention.

When a specific order of business is stated in the constitution or bylaws, and the assembly desires to take up business out of this fixed order, it may be done by a motion to suspend the rules. A question, motion, or item of business which has come before the assembly can be postponed temporarily or postponed definitely, but a whole class of business, such as unfinished business, cannot be postponed except by a motion to suspend the rules. Changes in the order of business are frequently made by unanimous consent.

## Specific Items under Order of Business

The secretary should provide the presiding officer with a detailed memorandum of each item to come up under each section of the order of business. The list under "unfinished business" should include all business incomplete when the previous meeting adjourned or any matter postponed to the current meeting. All items of business which have been specially set for consideration at a particular time, commonly called special orders, and the hour for their consideration should be listed. Under the heading "committee reports" all committees to be called upon for a report should be listed with the names of the chairmen. Announcements for the presiding officer to read should be written out in full, and the names of the members to be called upon to make announcements should be listed.

## Call to Order

The presiding officer should call a meeting to order promptly at the hour fixed for the meeting by rapping with his gavel and announcing:

"The meeting will please come to order,"

*or*

"The eighty-third Annual Convention of the Benevolent and Protective Order of Elks is now convened,"

*or*

by other appropriate statement.

## Reading of Minutes

After a meeting is called to order, the first step, unless a roll call is to be taken, is the reading of the minutes of the previous meeting.

The presiding officer calls upon the secretary to read the minutes by stating:

"The secretary will please read the minutes of the last meeting."

The reading of the minutes may be postponed or deferred by a majority vote, or if the organization has a standing committee on minutes, this committee corrects the minutes and reports at regular intervals. If the reading of the minutes of several previous meetings has been postponed, the chairman directs the secretary to read the minutes of all regular and special meetings held since the last reading of the minutes.

## Reports of Committees

The presiding officer next calls upon the chairman of each board or standing committee in the order in which it is named in the bylaws and asks if he has any report to make.

Then special committee chairmen are called upon in the order of their appointment.

At conventions the order of business, or agenda, frequently makes specific provisions for reports of particular committees. The order of committee reports necessarily is often determined by the order in which committees are ready to report, and an organization should not permit its business to be interfered with by a too rigid adherence to a fixed order of committee reports.

Committee reports are considered in detail in the chapter on Committees (see Chapter 18).

## Unfinished Business

The presiding officer may introduce this section of the order of business with the statement:

"Unfinished business is now in order."

The presiding officer then presents the first matter of unfinished business to the assembly for its consideration. For example, he may do this by saying:

"Discussion of the motion to send delegates to the International Conference at Antwerp was interrupted by adjournment. The secretary will please read this motion."

After the motion is read, the presiding officer may say:

"Discussion is now in order on the motion read by the secretary."

Unfinished business includes all business pending and undisposed of at the time of adjournment of the last meeting, as well as any matters postponed to the particular meeting or matters set as general orders for that day.

## New Business

When all unfinished business has been disposed of, the

presiding officer announces that new business is in order. He may say:

"New business is now in order. What is your pleasure?"

If no new business is presented, and the chairman knows of matters which should be acted upon, he should inform the assembly concerning them and ask if members wish to propose motions covering these matters.

## Announcements

When the time arrives for announcements, the presiding officer calls for announcements from members first and concludes with any which he wishes to make. The transaction of business is expedited by having a regular place in the order of business for announcements and requiring, so far as is practicable, that all announcements be confined to that time.

## Adjournment

The presiding officer should put the motion to adjourn to vote promptly, and if the motion carries he should immediately announce that "the meeting is adjourned." The meeting is not adjourned until the adjournment is announced.

# Chapter 3. QUORUM

## Quorum Necessary to Transact Business

A quorum is that number or proportion of the members of an organization who must be present at a meeting of the organization in order to legally transact business.[1] A presiding officer should not call a meeting to order in the absence of a quorum, except to vote to adjourn, after fixing the time for the next or adjourned meeting. Fewer than a quorum have an inherent right to adopt the motion to adjourn.[2]

## Number Necessary for Quorum

The number or proportion which constitutes a quorum of an organization is usually stated in its constitution or bylaws. In the absence of a provision which determines the quorum, common parliamentary law fixes the quorum at a majority of the members of the organization.[3]

It is legal and common practice for organizations to fix their quorum at less than a majority of the members.[4]

There are many organizations which rarely have a majority of their members present at regular meetings. These groups usually provide in the bylaws that a smaller number or proportion of the members constitutes a quorum.

In organizations with a fluctuating membership, it is wise to provide for a proportional number to constitute the quorum. Many organizations provide, for example, that one-fourth or one-sixth of the members shall constitute a quorum.

There are a few organizations, such as educational and religious groups, retaining members for life, which require a very small quorum. Many members seldom attend, and some of these groups provide in their rules that at any regular meeting the members present, regardless of their number, constitute a quorum.

In a convention a quorum is a majority of qualified delegates in attendance at the convention unless the bylaws provide otherwise.

A mass meeting, or an organization without a definite membership, counts the members present, no matter what their number, as a quorum.[5]

A committee requires a majority of its members for a quorum unless special provision is made for a different number.

When a quorum is fixed at a particular number, a reduction in the number of members of the organization does not alter the number constituting a quorum.[6]

## Computing a Quorum

In computing a quorum, only members in good standing are counted.[7] For example, the quorum of an organization with a membership list of 262 members and a required quorum of one-sixth of its members would be computed as follows:

| | |
|---|---:|
| Total membership list | 262 |
| Delinquent members | 12 |
| Members in good standing | 250 |
| Number required for quorum | 42 |

A quorum always refers to the number of members present and not to the number voting.[8] Thus, in the example just cited, if only 25 voted on a question, the vote would still be legal provided there was present a quorum of 42 or more members in good standing.

A member who is disqualified because of personal benefit or interest in a particular question cannot be counted for the purpose of computing a quorum for a vote on that question or of counting a majority of the quorum.[9] The presiding officer, if he is a member of the organization, is counted in computing a quorum.[10]

## Notice in Relation to Quorum

Since a majority of a quorum, which is often a very small proportion of the total membership, has the right and power to make decisions for the organization, rigid requirements for notices of meetings should be made in order that all members will have an opportunity to be present. Otherwise, a small group may make decisions that do not conform to the will of the majority. Some organizations which provide for a proportionately small quorum also require that members be notified of all important business to be transacted at meetings.

## Raising Question of Quorum

It is the right of any member who doubts at any time during a meeting that a quorum is present to request that the presence or absence of a quorum be determined. This request is in order at any time when no member is speaking. A direct inquiry is commonly stated as follows:

"Mr. Chairman, is there a quorum present?"

The older form of raising the question of the presence of a quorum was:

"Mr. Chairman, I suggest the absence of a quorum."

The presence of a quorum is determined by counting the members present or by calling the roll. The question as to the presence of a quorum cannot be raised repeatedly, when a quorum is obviously present, for the purpose of delaying business.

## Presumption of a Quorum

The courts hold that when it appears from the minutes that a quorum was present at a certain time during a meeting, and it does not appear that after that time there was an adjournment or recess, it will be presumed that the quorum continued to be present.[11] However, when a roll call shows that less than a quorum voted, it will not be presumed by the courts that a quorum continued to be present at the time the vote was taken.[12] The fact that a quorum was actually present at any particular time can be established by counting the members present or by entering on the roll the names of those present, regardless of whether they voted.

## Chapter 4. PRESENTATION OF MOTIONS

### Steps in Presenting a Motion

A motion, in its broad sense, is the formal statement of a proposal or question for consideration and action by an assembly. It presents an item of business for decision and may also be referred to as a "question" or "proposition."

The orderly presentation of a motion requires the following successive steps:

1. A member rises and addresses the presiding officer.
2. The member is recognized by the presiding officer.
3. The member proposes a motion.
4. Another member seconds the motion.
5. The presiding officer states the motion to the assembly.

The assembly may then consider the motion and debate it if it is a debatable motion.

### Addressing the Presiding Officer

Any member, except when presiding, has the right to present a motion. To do this, the member rises and addresses the presiding officer by his official title, for example, "Mr. President," "Madam Chairman," or "Mr. Moderator." If the presiding officer has no official title, it is always correct to address him as "Mr. Chairman" or if the presiding officer is a woman, as "Madam Chairman." This form of address signifies to the presiding officer that the member wishes to "obtain the floor," that is, to have the right to speak or to present a motion. After addressing the presiding officer, the member waits for recognition.

## Recognition by the Presiding Officer

All other things being equal, the first person who rises after the floor has been yielded and asks for recognition is entitled to speak. If several members seek recognition from the chairman at the same time, the following logical rules help him to decide which person should be recognized first:

1. Preference is given to the proposer of a motion (or a committee chairman who has presented a report), who is allowed the first opportunity to explain the motion or report.

2. A member who has not spoken has prior claim over one who has already discussed the question. Likewise, a member who seldom speaks is given preference over one who claims the attention of the assembly frequently.

3. When possible, the chairman alternates between proponents and opponents of a motion. In discussions where there are opposing opinions, the chairman may inquire of a speaker on which side he intends to speak and thus divide the opportunity to speak more equitably.

The chairman recognizes a member by announcing his name as "Mr. A" or if he does not know the name, as "Mr. Member" or "The delegate at the microphone in the center aisle" or by nodding to him or otherwise designating him. In large organizations and in conventions where the chairman does not know the names of all the members, the member, when he is recognized, states his name and the organization or district which he represents.

Having received formal recognition from the presiding officer, a member is said to "have the floor"; that is, he is entitled to speak or to present a motion. All other members who were seeking recognition from the chairman should be seated as soon as one member is recognized.

## Proposing a Motion

A motion is a proposal that the assembly take certain action or express certain sentiments. It should be stated in the form "I move that" (which means "I propose that") followed by a statement of the proposal which the member wishes to bring before the assembly; for example:

"I move that this organization purchase a site for a new headquarters building."

This is the only correct phraseology for proposing a motion. The forms "I move you" or " I make a motion" or, after some discussion, "I so move" are incorrect. Statements beginning "I propose" or "I suggest" should not be recognized as motions. Aside from occasional brief explanatory remarks, no discussion is permissible when a motion is being presented.

To ensure accuracy, it is desirable that the proposer of a lengthy motion write it out before proposing it. If the proposer of such a motion fails to do so, the chairman may request him to write it out for the secretary.

## Proposing a Resolution

If the proposal is one stating a sentiment or a formal expression of the opinion of the assembly, it is usually presented in the form of a resolution. Resolutions are always in writing and are used instead of motions when the statement is too long or too involved, or when the subject is too delicate to trust to an oral statement. Resolutions are usually introduced by the statement:

"I move the adoption of the following resolution."

A typical resolution may read as follows:

"*Resolved,* That this organization formally express its appreciation of the excellent service rendered by our retiring president during the past two years and that he be endorsed by this organization as a candidate for the State Executive Committee."

The old practice of prefacing resolutions with numerous statements, each introduced by the word "whereas," is almost obsolete. The statements contained in the "whereases" were of no legal effect and sometimes were the cause of disagreement. Members frequently questioned the truth of these prefacing statements and attempted to amend them and to debate them—often to the neglect of the resolving clause. Common modern practice presents the reasons for the adoption of a resolution in the form of debate, rather than in the introductory "whereases."

Resolutions are read by the secretary or by the member presenting them. In some instances a set of resolutions is presented to the secretary to be read, and when they have been read, some member moves that the resolutions as read be adopted. The member presenting a resolution may read it if he wishes and then hand it to the secretary.[1]

## Seconding a Motion

After a member has stated his motion, he resumes his seat, and it is then in order for another member to second the motion. The motion is seconded by another member saying, without waiting for recognition, "I second the motion." Seconding a motion indicates that the member wishes the matter to receive consideration by the assembly. As a general rule, every motion requires a second. In some deliberative bodies, including the Houses of Congress, it is provided by rule or established by custom that a motion does not require a second.

Routine motions, such as moving that a bill be paid, are frequently put to vote without waiting for a second. If anyone objects to the lack of a second, the presiding officer must call for a formal second.

If a motion is not promptly seconded, it may be that it is not clear to the members. In this case, the chairman should state the motion again and ask if there is a second, and if after waiting for a moment, there is no response, he may declare: "The motion is lost for want of a second" and proceed to other business.

*Statement of a Motion by the Presiding Officer*

When a motion has been properly moved and seconded, it is the duty of the chairman to state that motion to the assembly.

It is the duty of the presiding officer to state every motion as clearly as possible and in correct form even though he may have to change the wording of the motion. The presiding officer may not change the meaning of any motion in any particular, however, without the consent of its proposer. In case of any mistake by the presiding officer in stating a motion or in case of a difference of opinion as to the exact wording of a motion, it is the motion as stated by the proposing member rather than the motion as stated by the presiding officer which controls in determining the meaning.[2]

The presiding officer may state the motion in the following form:

"It has been moved and seconded that this organization establish a camp for the children of the North Beach area. Is there any discussion?"

*or*

"It has been moved and seconded that the following resolution be adopted:

Resolved, That this congregation commend the courageous action of our minister at the International Religious Council."

After a motion has been formally stated to the assembly, it belongs to the body and is no longer under the control of its proposer. From the time when it is formally stated by the presiding officer until it is voted upon, or otherwise disposed of by the assembly, it is open to debate and is known as the "pending question." When a motion is superseded by motions of higher precedence, the last motion stated by the chairman is the "immediately pending question."

## Example of Proper Presentation of a Motion

The following is an illustration of the steps necessary in presenting a motion:

MR. A [rising and addressing the presiding officer]: "Mr. Chairman."

CHAIRMAN: "Mr. A."

MR. A: "I move that this club undertake a campaign to raise funds for the purchase of the property adjoining our clubhouse."

MR. B [without rising]: "I second the motion."

CHAIRMAN: "It has been moved and seconded that this organization undertake a campaign to raise funds for the purchase of the property which adjoins our clubhouse. Is there any discussion?"

Discussion of the motion is then in order.

## Chapter 5. CLASSIFICATION OF MOTIONS

### Classes of Motions

Motions are classified according to their precedence and purpose into four groups. These groups, in the inverse order of their precedence, are:

1. Main motions
2. Subsidiary motions
3. Incidental motions
4. Privileged motions

### Main Motions

Main motions comprise the most important group. Their purpose is to bring business before an assembly in such a form that it may be discussed and acted upon. A general main motion may deal with any subject which a member may properly bring before an assembly.

There are several specialized main motions which have acquired a specific form and are subject to special rules. In this book they are referred to as "specific main motions" to indicate that they are main motions, although they are known by specific names.

Specific main motions have the precedence of general main

motions, but are individually governed by somewhat different rules.

The more common specific main motions are:

1. Reconsider
2. Rescind
3. Create orders
4. Resume consideration

The privileged motions and appeals have the characteristics of main motions and, if proposed when nothing is before the assembly, are treated as main motions; or, stated differently, they are main motions which have been given a higher precedence because of their urgency.

## Subsidiary Motions

Subsidiary motions are used to modify or dispose of the main motion. They are called subsidiary motions because they are subsidiary to the main motion and depend upon it for existence. They are really alternative aids in considering, acting upon, and disposing of the main motion. Since they relate to the main motion before the assembly, it is "in order" (correct from a parliamentary standpoint) to propose them when a main motion is pending before the assembly. The following seven subsidiary motions are listed in the order of their precedence:

1. Postpone temporarily (lay on the table)
2. Vote immediately (previous question)
3. Limit debate
4. Postpone definitely
5. Refer to a committee
6. Amend
7. Postpone indefinitely

There are two motions, commonly classified as incidental motions, which are really subsidiary in character because they can be used directly in disposing of a main motion.

These are the motion to withdraw a motion and the objection to consideration of a motion. The usual classification of these two motions as incidental is followed in this book.

## Incidental Motions

The incidental motions have few general characteristics in common except that they arise only incidentally out of the business before the assembly. Because of their nature incidental motions may come up at any time when they are needed. As a group they rank in precedence below privileged motions and above subsidiary motions. They have no order of precedence among themselves in the procedure of ordinary organizations, and it is only necessary that they be disposed of as soon as they arise and prior to the question out of which they arise. Most of the incidental motions are concerned with demands or requests relating to the rights of the members. The more frequently used incidental motions are:

1. Appeal
2. Point of order
3. Parliamentary inquiry
4. Suspend rules
5. Withdraw a motion
6. Object to consideration
7. Division of the question
8. Division of the assembly

There are a considerable number of other motions which come within the classification of incidental motions. They relate to the priority of consideration, to the manner of consideration, or to other incidental questions which may arise out of the consideration of another motion. Examples of this type of incidental motion are motions or requests to vote by ballot, to excuse a member from voting, and to consider a resolution paragraph by paragraph.

The purpose of this group of motions is to provide a means of reaching decisions on the many procedural questions which arise out of or as a result of the consideration of other questions and which must be decided before the questions out of which they arise.

These questions may be presented as either motions or requests. If proposed as requests, they are acted upon by unanimous consent. They cannot interrupt a speaker and cannot be amended or debated. When proposed as motions, they follow the same rules except that they require a second and a majority vote.

## Privileged Motions

Privileged motions have no direct connection with the main motion before the assembly but are emergency motions in that they are of such urgency that they are entitled to immediate consideration. They relate to the members and to the organization rather than to particular items of business. They are motions which, but for their urgency, would be main motions. Because of their immediate importance they are given the privilege of setting aside temporarily whatever motions of lower rank are before the assembly. Privileged motions are only privileged when other business is before the assembly. If made when there is no motion before the assembly, they are treated as main motions and are subject to all the rules applicable to main motions.

The privileged motions are:

1. Adjourn
2. Recess
3. Question of privilege

# Chapter 6. PRECEDENCE OF MOTIONS

## Order of Precedence

By precedence is meant the priority or order in which motions may be proposed, considered, and disposed of. The rules of precedence are definite and should present no difficulty.

The precedence in relation to main motions of the most frequently used motions is as follows:

    I. *Privileged Motions*
        1. Adjourn
        2. Recess
        3. Question of privilege
   II. *Incidental Motions* (Incidental motions have no order of precedence among themselves.)
  III. *Subsidiary Motions*
        4. Postpone temporarily (lay on the table)
        5. Vote immediately (previous question)
        6. Limit debate
        7. Postpone definitely
        8. Refer to a committee
        9. Amend
      10. Postpone indefinitely
  IV. *Main Motions*
      11. Main motions and specific main motions

## Rules of Precedence

There are two basic rules of precedence. The first is that when a motion is pending, any motion of higher precedence may be proposed but no motion of lower precedence may be proposed. In the preceding list of motions, the motion to adjourn (No. 1) has the highest rank, whereas a main motion (No. 11) has the lowest. For example, when motion No. 8 in the list is pending, a member may propose motion No. 6 but not motion No. 10. The second rule is that motions are considered and voted upon in inverse order to their proposal, the last proposed being considered and disposed of first. For example, if motions 11, 9, 7, and 4 were proposed in that order and were all pending, they would be taken up for consideration in the inverse order: 4, 7, 9, and 11.

Incidental motions have no order of precedence among themselves in ordinary organizations, but as a group they have precedence between privileged and subsidiary motions. Since they arise incidentally out of the business before the assembly and are decided as soon as they arise, they present no problem of precedence.

## Example of Precedence

Suppose that a member proposes a main motion "that all members of the Chamber of Commerce be assessed five dollars for the Christmas Fund." This main motion is No. 11 in the Chart of Precedence. While this motion is pending, another member moves to amend it by striking out the word "five" and inserting the word "ten" (No. 9). While this amendment is being discussed, a member moves to "refer the matter to a committee" (No. 8). While the propriety of reference to a committee is being considered, someone moves to postpone discussion of the original motion until the next meeting (No. 7). A member then moves to postpone the question indefinitely (No. 10). A member rises to the point of order that the motion "to postpone indefinitely" is out of order because it is of lower precedence than the immediately pending question (No. 7). This point of order is an incidental motion and therefore must be decided at once. The chairman rules the member's point "well taken" and states that the motion to postpone indefinitely is not in order. He then states that the pending question is the motion to postpone until the next meeting. A member then moves to "take a recess" (No. 2). All of these motions, except the one ruled out of order, have followed correct precedence and are in order. Five motions are then before the assembly, and the highest in order of precedence must be acted upon before the next in order can be taken up. The order of precedence of the pending motions is as follows:

| *Motions Pending* | *Order of Precedence* |
|---|---|
| Recess | 2 |
| Postpone definitely | 7 |
| Refer to a committee | 8 |
| Amendment | 9 |
| Main motion | 11 |

The chairman first takes a vote on the motion to recess. If it is lost, he calls for discussion on the motion to postpone to the next meeting. If this motion loses, he states the motion to refer the motion to a committee. If this motion carries, the whole matter, including the amendment, is referred to the committee. If it loses, the chairman asks for discussion on the amendment. When the amendment has been voted upon, he calls for discussion on the main question. At any point motions of a higher precedence than the one under consideration could be proposed.

Such a complicated problem of precedence occurs rarely.

However, it is quite possible for several motions to be awaiting decision by the assembly at one time. All motions which have been proposed but not yet decided are known as "pending questions." The particular motion which is under consideration by the assembly at a particular time is known as the "immediately pending question." It is the duty of the chairman, with the aid of the secretary, to keep the assembly clearly informed as to what motion is immediately pending.

# Chapter 7. RULES GOVERNING MOTIONS

*Rules Applicable to All Motions*

Orderly procedure requires that when a motion has acquired a particular form and particular rules governing it, these rules be strictly applied. One of the essential requirements of parliamentary law is that rules be so definite that their effect is known in advance. Nothing is more essential to procedure, in which full justice is accorded each member, than that all rules be applied with uniformity and certainty.

It is better to understand thoroughly the purpose of each motion and the fundamental principles of procedure governing motions, and thus to be able to reason out for oneself what rules apply to a particular motion, than to attempt to memorize all of the individual rules governing each motion. Familiarity in use of the rules is acquired with practice.

The rules governing motions are, for the most part, logical and, once reasoned out, self-evident. The questions which one needs to be able to answer concerning each motion are:

1. Can the motion interrupt a speaker?
2. Does the motion require a second?
3. Is the motion debatable?
4. Can the motion be amended?

5. What vote does the motion require?
6. What is the precedence of the motion?
7. To what motions can the motion apply?
8. What motions can be applied to the motion?
9. Can the motion be renewed?

The answers to the nine questions concerning each motion differ but may be grouped and summarized under a few determining rules. Such a summary provides a general background for deciding what rules govern each motion and will help in remembering the rules without reference to a chart.

## Can the Motion Interrupt a Speaker?

Ordinarily a speaker, once recognized, is entitled to the floor so long as he does not violate any of the rules of decorum. It is the duty of the presiding officer to protect him in that right.

Because of their urgency a few motions are permitted to interrupt a speaker. These motions are of two types: those which are subject to a time limit and those which present a question requiring immediate attention. Motions of the first type must be proposed, considered, and decided within a specific time limit. If delayed beyond such a specific limit, they are too late to receive consideration.

The four motions of this type are:
1. Reconsider
2. Object to consideration
3. Appeal
4. Division of the assembly

The motion to reconsider a vote must be made on the day the vote was taken or on the next business day of a convention. If it is not made within this time it cannot be made at all. Therefore it is necessary that the motion to reconsider be permitted to interrupt a speaker.

An appeal and a demand for a division of the assembly

must be made before other business intervenes and for that reason may interrupt a speaker.

The second type of motion which may interrupt a speaker are those relating to the immediate rights and privileges of a member or of the organization itself.

The motions of this type are:

1. Question of privilege
2. Point of order
3. Parliamentary inquiry

A question of privilege involving the immediate convenience, comfort, or rights of the organization or its members may arise during a speech. Frequently the question of privilege is so urgent that it must be permitted to interrupt the speaker. For example, a draft from an open window might cause acute discomfort and a member should be allowed to interrupt a speaker with a question of privilege, requesting that the window be closed.

A point of order involving a mistake or error or failure to comply with the rules must often be raised during a speech. To interrupt a speaker, a point of order must relate to the speech itself, to the speaker, or to some question which cannot properly await the completion of the speech for its determination.

A parliamentary inquiry is very similar to a point of order in that it may raise a question as to present procedure or procedure which might be immediately taken. Therefore, it must relate to the speaker or the subject he is discussing or some other matter which cannot properly be delayed until the completion of the speech.

## Does the Motion Require a Second?

Motions normally require seconds. This requirement is based on the principle that any proposal, to be of sufficient interest to justify the attention of the assembly, should have the support of at least two members: one who makes the motion and another who indicates his support of the proposal, or his willingness to consider it, by a second.

There are, however, a number of actions which do not require seconds. This is because they are not technically motions, although for convenience they are classified as motions. Whenever a member is given a right or privilege, either by parliamentary law or by the rules of the organization, he can assert that right through the use of demands, requests, points of order, or inquiries.

The following do not require seconds:

1. Point of order
2. Parliamentary inquiry
3. Division of assembly
4. Division of a question
5. Object to consideration
6. Withdraw a motion
7. Question of privilege

When a question of privilege requires a decision by the assembly instead of by the presiding officer, it is properly presented as a motion and, consequently, requires a second.

Frequently requests such as requests to withdraw a motion, or for unanimous consent, do not meet with unanimous approval, and it becomes necessary to present the question of granting or refusing the request to the assembly for its determination. The question then is presented as a motion and consequently requires a second.

## Is the Motion Debatable?

The following motions only are fully debatable:

1. Main motion
2. Amendment (unless applied to an undebatable motion)
3. Postpone indefinitely
4. Appeal
5. Reconsider
6. Rescind

The business of an organization is largely conducted through main motions which present matters of business for determination. These are substantive propositions requiring the consideration and deliberation of the organization and must, therefore, be debatable. Amendments to main motions present questions of the same nature and actually involve portions or features of the main motion itself and, likewise, are subject to full debate and consideration.

The motion to postpone indefinitely is debatable and opens the main question to debate. This is true because the motion to postpone indefinitely is, in fact, the main motion presented in negative form and is equivalent to a motion to reject.[1] If it receives an affirmative vote, it finally disposes of the main motion. It is, therefore, debatable and opens the main question to debate.

An appeal from the decision of the chair is debatable because the effect of the motion is to transfer the responsibilities for the decision from the presiding officer to the assembly. It is necessary that the presiding officer be permitted to give the reason for his decision and that those interested in the appeal be able to present their reasons for the appeal before the assembly can decide whether or not the decision of the presiding officer should be upheld.

Motions to reconsider and rescind are debatable because they reopen the main question to debate.

Three motions are subject to restricted debate. These are the motions to postpone definitely, to create orders, and to refer to a committee. Debate on the motion to postpone definitely is restricted to the advisability of postponing the consideration of a main motion or to the time to which the motion is to be postponed. Debate on the motion to make a main motion or a subject an order which must be considered at a particular time is restricted to the suitability or unsuitability of the proposed time for consideration. Debate on the motion to refer a motion or subject to a committee is restricted to the following:

1. The advisability of referring the matter to a committee
2. The method of selecting the committee
3. The number of committee members
4. Instructions to the committee

None of these three motions permitting restricted debate opens the main question to debate.

Debate is not permitted on other motions because they deal with procedure and therefore can be decided without debate.

## Can the Motion Be Amended?

A simple test determines whether a motion can be amended: Is the motion variable in form? If it can be varied in wording, it can be amended.

For example, the motion "I move we recess for ten minutes" could as well have been stated, "I move we recess for fifteen minutes." Motions which may be varied in form are necessarily amendable in order that they can be made to express the will of the majority.

On the other hand, a motion which is not variable in form cannot be amended. The motion to postpone indefinitely, for example, can be stated in only one form and, therefore, cannot be amended.

The only motions which can be freely amended are:

1. Main motions
2. Amendments

Four motions can be varied only as to time and, therefore, can be amended only as to time. These motions are:

1. Postpone definitely
2. Limit debate
3. Recess
4. Create orders

The motion to refer to a committee may be amended as to the name of the committee, number of members, and the method of their selection, or it may be amended to give instructions to a committee.

Requests, points of order, or demands cannot be amended. They are not technically motions since they do not present questions to the assembly for its determination. This group includes:

1. Points of order
2. Appeal
3. Parliamentary inquiry
4. Division of the assembly
5. Division of a question
6. Objections to consideration
7. Request to withdraw a motion

## What Vote Does the Motion Require?

The theory of democratic government rests upon control by the majority. This same concept is the foundation of parliamentary procedure. Basically, all motions require a majority vote. The requirement of a two-thirds vote to take certain actions was unknown to the common law. It was not a part of early parliamentary practice; and it is today not universal in its use in legislative practice.

The present practice of requiring a two-thirds vote to limit or prevent debate or take up questions out of their regular order has so long been followed in ordinary non-governmental organizations that it may now be said to have acquired the status of a parliamentary rule. The theoretical basis of the rule is that motions which set aside fundamental principles require more than a majority vote in order that the minority may be protected. Under this principle the motions listed on the following page require a two-thirds vote:

1. Vote immediately (previous question)
2. Limit debate
3. Suspend the rules
4. Object to consideration

The motions to vote immediately (previous question) and to limit debate require a two-thirds vote because they set aside or restrict the right of unlimited debate.

The motion to suspend the rules requires a two-thirds vote because it permits a deviation from the usual required procedure, and a vote of more than a majority is necessary to protect the minorities, which may be affected adversely by the motion.

Objection to consideration requires a two-thirds vote because members ordinarily have the privilege of presenting any matter for discussion which they consider appropriate. A two-thirds vote is consequently required to take away that privilege.

## What Is the Precedence of the Motion?

To avoid confusion, it is necessary to assign a priority or rank to each motion. This priority is based on the urgency of the action which each motion presents. Motions are listed in the order of their precedence on the inside front cover of this book. When a motion is before the assembly, any motion is in order which has a higher precedence or rank than the pending motion, but no motion is in order which has a lower precedence than the pending motion.

The general order of precedence gives privileged motions the highest rank, subsidiary motions second, and main and specific main motions the lowest. Incidental motions have no individual precedence, but as a group they rank between privileged and subsidiary motions. They may be proposed at any time they are needed and are decided immediately.

## To What Motions Can the Motion Apply?

A motion is said to apply to another motion when it is used to alter or dispose of the original motion. For example, if a main motion "to make a survey of fire insurance rates in this city" is being considered and a member moves "to postpone further consideration of the motion until Friday at three o'clock," the motion to postpone definitely is said to "apply to" the main motion.

*Privileged motions* relate to the organization and its members rather than to particular items of business and do not, therefore, apply to any other motions.

*Incidental motions* relate generally to the order or manner of considering business. They do not apply to other motions, except: that the motion to withdraw can apply to any motion, that objection to consideration can apply to main motions only, and that division of a question can apply to main motions and amendments.

*Subsidiary motions* all apply to main motions. The motions to vote immediately (previous question) and to limit debate naturally apply to all debatable motions. The motion to amend can apply to any motion which is variable in form.

*Main motions* can apply to no other motions.

*Specific main motions* apply only to main motions, except that the motion to reconsider can apply to amendments and appeals.

## What Motions Can Be Applied to the Motion?

When a motion is being considered, it is very important to know what motions can be applied to it. A few rules determine what motions may be applied to each individual motion. These rules are:

1. Every motion can have the motion to withdraw applied to it.

2. The privileged motions and the incidental motions can have no other motions than withdraw applied to them, except that recess may be amended and an appeal is subject to motions to close or limit debate and may be reconsidered.

3. All debatable motions can have the motions to vote immediately or limit debate applied to them.

4. All motions which may be stated in more than one way (which are variable in form) can be amended.

5. Main motions can have all the subsidiary motions applied to them, and, in addition, are subject to object to consideration, reconsider, and withdraw. Amendments can have the same motions applied to them with the exception of object to consideration.

## Can the Motion Be Renewed?

When a motion has been voted upon by an assembly and that motion is lost, it cannot be renewed except under certain conditions.

When a motion must be presented immediately after a situation arises, if it is to be presented at all, it is obvious that it cannot be renewed. Therefore objection to consideration, appeal, point of order, and call for division cannot be renewed.

Certain actions which are broadly classified as motions but which are really requests, inquiries, or privileges and which are not decided by vote logically cannot be renewed. These include a question of privilege and a request for division of a question (unless made in the form of a motion) and a parliamentary inquiry.

Procedural motions cannot be renewed unless there has been a change in the parliamentary situation which, in effect, makes the renewed motion a new question. Change in the parliamentary situation means intervening business or progress in debate or other changes which create a new situation so that the assembly might reasonably take a different position on the question to be renewed.[2] The following procedural motions can be renewed only after a change in the parliamentary situation: adjourn, recess, suspend rules, withdraw a motion, postpone temporarily, vote immediately, limit debate, postpone definitely, refer to a committee, resume consideration, and create orders.

Main motions which have been rejected, postponed indefinitely, or concerning which an objection to consideration has been sustained cannot be renewed, but may be introduced at a future meeting or convention as a new motion.

An amendment which has been defeated cannot be renewed at the same meeting or convention.

The motion to postpone indefinitely (which is a negative form of the main motion) cannot be renewed. The motions to reconsider and rescind are themselves forms of a second consideration of a motion and consequently cannot be renewed.

# Chapter 8. DEBATE

## Right to Debate

The object of deliberative bodies is to reach the mature judgment and decision of the group by means of free interchange of thought and discussion.

The right of every member to be heard, to participate fully in the discussion of any matter of business which comes before the assembly, is one of the fundamental principles of parliamentary law.[1] The right to debate is regulated by parliamentary rules in order to assure every member a reasonable and equal opportunity to debate. A knowledge of the rules governing debate is, therefore, essential to every member to enable him to exercise his rights fully.[2]

## Extent of Debate

All motions can be classified into three groups according to the extent of debate permitted on them. These are:

1. Undebatable motions
2. Motions open to restricted debate
3. Motions open to full debate

Most undebatable motions are simple procedural motions which can be decided without discussion. The motions to postpone a motion temporarily (lay on the table) or to vote immediately (previous question) are examples of undebatable motions.

Motions which are open to restricted debate may require brief, restricted discussion before a member can vote intelligently upon them. The motion to refer to a committee, for example, may require restricted discussion as to the advisability of the question's being referred to a committee or as to the personnel or powers or method of selection of the committee or as to instructions to be given to the committee. However, debate is limited strictly to these details and cannot extend to the merits of the main question.

Motions open to full debate are those which may require unlimited discussion for their decision. A main motion is a good example of a fully debatable motion. In addition to main motions there are only three fully debatable motions: amend (if applied to a debatable motion), appeal, and postpone indefinitely.

## Obtaining the Floor for Debate

As soon as a motion has been stated to the assembly by the presiding officer, any member has a right to discuss it after "obtaining the floor." The member waits until the floor has been "yielded" (given up by the preceding speaker), then rises and addresses the presiding officer and waits for recognition. He obtains the floor in the same manner as when presenting a motion (see page 18).

When a member is recognized, he is entitled to protection in his exclusive right to be heard so long as he conforms to the rules of debate.

## Relevancy in Debate

One of the most important principles of debate is that all

discussion must be relevant to the subject which is before the assembly. Any member granted the floor has been given it only for the purpose of discussing the pending question, and if he departs from that subject, he is out of order. In discussing a point, a member may use illustrations or tell a story so long as he does not digress from the question. If the speaker digresses from the subject, the presiding officer should interrupt him and request that he confine his remarks to the question. If the chairman fails to interrupt a speaker who is irrelevant in his discussion, any member may rise to a point of order and call the attention of the chairman to the speaker's digression. The chairman must then direct the speaker to confine his discussion to the question before the assembly.

Discussion is always restricted to the immediately pending motion. When a motion is under discussion and a motion of higher precedence is made, discussion is directed to the motion of higher precedence until it is decided. For example, when an amendment is proposed to a motion under discussion, debate must be confined to the amendment until it is disposed of. Debate then reverts to the motion.

## What Is Not Debate

An inquiry or suggestion is not debate and is not subject to the rules limiting debate. Every member, before voting on any question, is entitled to know precisely what the question is and what its effects will be. A member is entitled to have a question restated before voting or at any time when there may be uncertainty as to the question. He is entitled to ask for an explanation of a question or to raise a parliamentary inquiry, and it is proper for the presiding officer to permit an occasional brief suggestion, even with relation to an undebatable motion.

## Members' Conduct during Debate

Debate must be fundamentally impersonal. All debate is addressed to the presiding officer rather than to the members and must never be directed to any individual. Officers are referred to by their official titles instead of by name. Members are designated by some phrase such as "the last speaker," "the member who preceded me," or "the delegate from Texas." The purpose of these forms of address is to eliminate personalities and to conform to the maxim that "measures, not men, are discussed by assemblies."

It is never permissible to attack the motives of a member but a motion or its nature or consequences may be attacked and condemned. It is the motion, not its advocate, that is the subject of debate.

Arguments and opinions should be stated as clearly and precisely as possible. The speaker should remember that he is talking, not for his own pleasure nor for the entertainment of others, but to assist the assembly in arriving at a conclusion on the question under discussion. Adherence to this principle ensures real progress in debate.

A member's effectiveness in debate is influenced by the courtesy with which he treats the presiding officer and other members. If a member should so far forget his dignity as to use improper language or conduct himself in a disorderly manner, he should be promptly called to order by the chairman or by some other member rising to a point of order. When the speaker is called to order by another member, he must be seated until the point of order is decided by the chairman. If a member fails or refuses to conduct his discussion in an orderly and courteous manner, he may be refused the right to the floor. If necessary, he may be ejected from the meeting by order of the presiding officer or by vote of the assembly.

## Presiding Officer's Duties during Debate

The presiding officer has an obligation both to the speaker and to the other members to control and expedite debate. When a member has been assigned the floor, he has the right to the quiet and undivided attention of the assembly so long as he conducts himself properly and does not exceed any limits which may have been fixed for debate. It is the duty of the presiding officer to protect the speaker in this right, to suppress disorder, to eliminate whispering and walking about, and to prevent any annoyance or heckling or unnecessary interruption. It is also his duty to keep the subject clearly before the members and to rule out any irrelevant discussion and to restate the question whenever necessary. For the welfare of the organization the chairman should insist upon the attention of every member to the business before the assembly. The assembly owes respectful attention to the presiding officer and to each speaker.

## Time Limits for Debate

It is customary in some organizations to fix a time limit for debate in the bylaws or rules. Each assembly has the right to fix limits as to the length of speeches or debate.

Parliamentary law fixes no definite limit on the length of speeches. An early writer attempted to set an arbitrary limit of ten minutes for each speech by parliamentary rule but this limit has not been accepted in practice.

Debate can ordinarily be kept within reasonable time limits by the chairman's insistence that all debate conform strictly to the point under discussion.

## Cutting Off Debate

It is unwise to make a practice of cutting off or preventing debate and deliberation on debatable questions. This is true whether debate is cut off by recognized motions or by arbitrarily bringing questions to vote without adequate opportunity for discussion. Members cannot be expected to maintain the interest and support necessary to the proper functioning of an organization if denied the right to participate freely in its deliberations. Since full discussion of all proposals is a fundamental right of members, a motion which restricts or sets aside this right by closing or limiting debate requires a two-thirds vote.[3]

## Bringing a Question to Vote

When it appears to the chairman that all of the members who wish to speak have done so, he should inquire:

"Is there any further discussion?"

*or*

"Are you ready for the question?"

The proper response to these queries is not to call out "Question!" but to remain silent unless one wishes to discuss the motion.

These queries give notice to members that if they desire to speak, they must claim the right immediately. If no one responds to the queries, the chairman puts the question to vote.

The chairman should never hurry the vote and should pause after the query, "Are you ready for the question?" Prematurely putting the question to vote, however, does not cut off the right of members to speak. A member, if reasonably prompt in claiming the privilege, can assert his right to debate at any time before the taking of the vote is completed and the result announced. If there is discussion after an affirmative vote is taken, the chairman must call for the affirmative vote again, since voters may have changed their opinions during the discussion. Debate is finally and completely closed by the announcement of the vote.

## The Proposer of a Motion and Debate

When a member has proposed a motion, given a committee report, or presented other business to the assembly, he has a prior right to the floor to explain the motion or report and to present his reasons for its support. To exercise that right, he must request recognition promptly. The proposer or some other advocate of a motion is usually permitted to close the debate on the question.

## Informal Consideration

There are times when it is desirable to set aside the formal rules governing discussion and debate and to consider a subject informally. Informal consideration permits more freedom in the length and number of speeches. It also allows amendments and motions to be discussed simultaneously and gives broader latitude in debate.

Sometimes an assembly wishes to create a policy or plan which is not sufficiently understood or formulated to enable a member to propose a clear and adequate motion covering it. Time may not permit referring the problem to a committee. Rather than offer a poorly thought-out motion, which will take considerable effort to perfect by amendment and which may lead to numerous technical difficulties, it is better to propose that the problem "be considered informally." For example, a member may rise and state: "We realize that some action must be taken to raise more funds for this organization. I move that we consider the problem of fund raising informally." If the motion for informal consideration carries, the chairman opens the problem for informal discussion. As soon as the question is clarified, a member should offer a motion embodying the plan. The vote on this motion is taken in the usual manner.

As soon as the motion or question requiring informal consideration has been disposed of, either temporarily or permanently, informal consideration automatically ceases without any motion or vote, and the regular rules of debate apply.

Informal consideration is a more satisfactory method of providing for informal debate than the old method of resolving the assembly into a "committee of the whole" and then formulating a report. Informal consideration also permits the regular chairman to continue to preside, whereas under the "committee of the whole" it is necessary to select a new chairman.

There are times in most organizations when it is possible to minimize technicalities and to expedite business by proceeding informally.

# Chapter 9. VOTE REQUIRED FOR

## LEGAL ACTIONS

## Majority Vote

The most fundamental rule governing voting is that at least a majority vote is required to take action. Jefferson referred to the ancient rule, *Lex Majoris Partis*. Until a majority has spoken, nothing is to be changed. It is obvious that to permit less than a majority to decide for any group would subject the many to the rule of the few and would be repugnant to the most basic democratic principle. That the majority must rule is universally accepted among democratic peoples.

## Importance of Defining Majority

Many important decisions are affected by widely varying interpretations of the term "majority vote." The problem of determining the vote required on each occasion is one of the most vital in the field of parliamentary law. It is also one of the most confused. For years parliamentary writers have talked about a "majority vote" with no clear or definite understanding of its many and varied meanings. There has been no parliamentary source which gives a complete statement of the different meanings of this important term. This confusion has resulted in hundreds of cases getting into court for the judge to decide which particular majority vote is meant. Even the judges of the Supreme Court of the United States have differed in at least one important case as to the meaning of the term "majority vote." [1]

## Kinds of Majority Vote

A majority vote may mean any of the following:

1. A majority of all the members
2. A majority of the positions or memberships in organizations having a fixed membership
3. A majority of the members present
4. A majority of a quorum
5. A majority of the total votes cast
6. A majority of the legal votes cast

If in an organization of 200 members, in which the quorum is one-quarter of the members, if there are 150 present and only 21 vote and 10 votes are not legal, a majority vote would be variously computed as follows:

1. A majority of all the members .............. 101
2. A majority of the members present ............ 76
3. A majority of a quorum ..................... 26
4. A majority of the total vote cast .............. 11
5. A majority of the legal votes cast ........... 6

The situation would be further complicated if this were an organization such as a country club, a stock exchange, or a legislative body with a fixed membership but with vacancies. Then the majority required could be either a majority of the entire membership, including vacancies, or a majority of the members at that time but excluding vacancies. If this type of organization had no rule defining the kind of majority required, the majority of the legal votes cast would bind the organization.

## One Vote May Be a Majority

Under certain circumstances a majority may consist of only one vote. Assume that some member brings up a question of such a nature that the members are confused about it or do not care to become involved or are perhaps not interested. When the chairman calls for the vote, the person sponsoring the question votes "aye" and no one votes "no." What is the result? The question is carried because it received the majority of the legal votes cast. A single affirmative vote, when there were no other votes cast, has been held by the courts to carry a question on the principle that it is a majority of the votes cast.

## Majority of the Members

When a majority vote of all the members is required, this means a vote of a majority of all the members both present and absent.[2] Thus if there are 80 members, a vote of 41 is necessary to take any action. If all 80 members are present, the vote of only a majority of the members present is required to carry a question, but if there are 41 present, a unanimous vote of those present is required. Under this rule a decision cannot be made for the organization by less than a majority of the members. A majority of all members is often required in organizations where the members act in a representative capacity.

## Majority of the Memberships

In organizations having a fixed membership, a majority of all the memberships or positions is often required to take an action. When this rule is applied to a city council of eight members, a majority is five, but if there are two vacancies reducing the actual number of members to six, the required vote is still five because a majority of the eight positions of the council is necessary.[3] This type of majority is frequently required in city councils, boards of supervisors, and other small bodies where members are acting in a representative capacity.

## Majority Vote of the Members Present

The vote of a majority of the members present is some-times required to take an action. Under this rule the failure of some members to vote does not reduce the number of affirmative votes required. If there are 304 members present an affirmative vote of 153 is necessary to act, regardless of the number voting. A failure to vote has the same effect as a "no" vote. Unless there is a requirement that all members who are present must vote, it is more reasonable to follow the usual rule and require only a majority of those voting.

## Majority of a Quorum

A majority of the quorum or a majority of the number who are authorized to do business for the organization is logically the minimum number which should be permitted to make decisions for all of the members in most business organizations. This is usually a majority of a majority. When there are sixty members and the quorum is a majority, the quorum would be thirty-one and the majority of a quorum would be sixteen. This number of affirmative votes cannot be reduced by the failure of members to vote.

## Majority of the Legal Votes Cast

When no other type of majority is specified, the common law provides that a majority of the legal votes cast is required. Only legal votes are to be counted unless the rules specify that the total vote cast is to be used as the basis for determining the vote required. An explanation of illegal votes is found on page 56.

A disadvantage of relying on a majority of the legal votes cast is that a very small number will often make the decisions for the organization. Decisions are much more likely to represent the will of the organization if they are made by a majority of those present or a majority of a quorum.

The legal theory under which the decisions of an organization may be made by a majority of those voting, even though less than a majority of a quorum, is that all the members have the right to vote if they wish to exercise the right. The members who fail to vote are presumed to have waived the exercise of their right and to have consented to allow the will of the organization to be expressed by those voting.[4]

To require more than a majority of the legal votes cast in organizations which cannot compel members to attend and to vote would often result in the organization's being unable to secure the vote necessary to act.

When, on a vote by ballot, more than one question is voted upon at a time, the votes cast on each question are computed separately, and a majority of the legal votes cast on that particular question is required.

## Bylaws Should Define Majority

Every organization should state in its bylaws the number of votes required on important decisions, just as it states the number necessary to constitute a quorum. If the required number is a majority, that word must be defined since a majority may mean anything from one vote to the majority of the total membership.

Some of the important questions on which organizations may wish to require more than a majority of the legal votes cast are:

1. Adoption of the budget
2. Sale, pledging, or purchase of property of organization
3. Dissolution of organization
4. Changes in organization policy
5. Change in custody of funds
6. Expulsion of members
7. Amendment of constitution and bylaws

## Illegal Votes, Void and Blank Ballots

An illegal vote in the strict sense is a vote cast by a person not entitled to vote, but in determining the number of legal votes cast, all votes are classed as "illegal" which are void or which for any reason cannot be counted.

A vote is void if it is not intelligible or if it is for an ineligible candidate or if for some like reason it cannot be counted.

When voting by ballot, members sometimes cast blank ballots when they do not wish to vote or to disclose that they are not voting on a question or for a candidate for office. Blank ballots naturally cannot be counted either for or against a question or candidate. A blank ballot is not to be regarded as a vote on any question and may be counted only to determine the presence of a quorum.

## A Tie Vote

A tie vote means that an equal number have voted in the affirmative and in the negative on a question or for opposing candidates. A tie vote does not decide a question because nothing is changed except by at least a majority of the legal votes cast. If the presiding officer has not voted and is a member of the organization, he may vote to break the tie.[5] If he is not a member of the organization, he cannot vote, except when specifically authorized to do so by the bylaws.[6] If he has already voted as a member of the organization, he cannot cast a second vote to break a tie unless this right is expressly given to him by the bylaws.[7]

## A Plurality Vote

A plurality vote is a vote of at least one vote more than the number received by any opposing candidate or measure. It arises only when there are three or more candidates or alternative propositions. The candidate, or measure, receiving the highest number of votes has a plurality. A tellers' report might show:

| Candidate | Votes |
|-----------|-------|
| A | 23 |
| B | 22 |
| C | 21 |
| Total | 66 |

The first candidate has a plurality vote, although no candidate has received a majority vote. A plurality vote does not elect a candidate nor carry a proposition except when there is a special rule of the organization to that effect.

## A Two-thirds Vote

A two-thirds vote means two-thirds of the legal votes cast unless it is qualified in some way, such as two-thirds of those present or of the total membership. Motions which prevent consideration of a motion or restrict debate on it or suspend rules or authorize variation from the usual order of business require a two-thirds vote because they infringe upon the fundamental right of a member to introduce motions and to have them discussed fully and in regular order.

## When a Member Does Not Vote

While it is almost always the right and usually the duty of every member to vote upon every question, in ordinary assemblies he cannot be compelled to vote upon every question.

As a general principle, no one should vote upon a question in which he has a direct personal or pecuniary interest.[8] For example, a member cannot legally vote on a motion awarding a contract to himself. The courts have recognized an exception to this rule when the organization itself is permitted and authorized to fix the compensation of its members. Otherwise, it would be impossible to vote to fix the compensation.[9] A member may vote on a question involving the whole organization when others are joined with him or affected by the vote, even though he has a direct personal or pecuniary interest. For example, every member has the right to vote on a motion authorizing the payment of mileage or other expenses.

When charges have been preferred against a member, he, naturally, cannot vote on the charges, but he may vote on charges if others are joined in them. Otherwise, a small proportion of members could gain control by filing charges against their opponents.

A member who has been nominated for office in an ordinary organization may vote for himself or, as a matter of courtesy, may cast his vote for an opponent. When a salary is involved, elections have been declared illegal when a member has voted for himself and that vote was necessary to his election.

## Actions Which Are Not Legal

Actions on the following questions, even though unanimous, are never legal:

1. A motion that conflicts with the laws of the nation, state, or city or with the constitution or bylaws of the organization.
2. Any motion forcing a member to reveal his opinions

on a question which is to be, or has been, voted upon by secret ballot. For example, a motion to make such a vote unanimous is illegal unless this motion is itself voted upon by ballot.

3. A rule protecting absentees can never be waived or suspended, as for example, a requirement included in the bylaws regarding notices for special meetings. In some instances, and often in the case of corporations, a required notice can be waived if all persons entitled to such notice sign a waiver or if all members of the organization are present.

# Chapter 10. METHODS AND PROCEDURE

## OF VOTING

### Voting Is a Fundamental Right

A member of any democratic body has the right to express his will or preference in electing officers and in deciding propositions. The right to have a voice in determining the will of an organization is the most fundamental right of a member. The will of an assembly is determined by taking a vote.[1]

### Methods of Voting

A vote may be taken by any of the following methods:

1. *Viva Voce* or *Voice Vote*. The chairman asks all those in favor of a motion to say "Aye" and those opposed, "No," and determines the prevailing side by the volume of voices. This is the most common manner of voting.

2. *Rising Vote*. First those in favor and then those opposed to a motion are asked to rise and are estimated or counted. This is the method used to verify an indecisive voice vote or to verify the vote after a call for a division.

3. *Counting* or *Show of Hands*. This method is similar to a rising vote but is sometimes more convenient.

4. *Tellers.* Those for and those against a motion pass between tellers, and the affirmative and negative vote is counted separately. This method is now rarely used.

5. *Roll Call (by "Yeas" and "Nays").* The names of those eligible to vote are called in alphabetical order, or by districts, and the members vote by saying "Yes" or "No" or "Aye" or "No" or "Yea" or "Nay," as their names are called. This method is used when it is desired to preserve the voting record of the individual members. It is particularly appropriate when members are voting in a representative capacity. This method is slower but more accurate than the preceding four methods.

6. *Ballot.* Each member records his vote by use of a paper ballot or some mechanical device. Vote by ballot is most frequently used in electing officers or voting upon amendments to a constitution or bylaws. When a vote is taken by ballot, several candidates or questions can be voted upon at the same time. This is the slowest method, but has the advantage of enabling members to keep their votes secret.

7. *Voting by Mail.* The constitution and bylaws may authorize voting by mail when it is impossible to vote by any of the more usual methods. Voting by mail is permitted only as specifically authorized.

8. *Unanimous Consent.* In addition to these methods of voting an assembly may act by unanimous consent. This is not actually a method of voting but of agreeing on a decision in the absence of objection by any member.

## Voice Vote

A question may be put to a voice vote as follows: "Those in favor of the motion say, 'Aye.' . . . Those opposed say, 'No.' . . ." If there is no doubt in the mind of the chairman as to the result of the vote, he announces it immediately by stating, "The motion is carried" or "The motion is lost."

A presiding officer never calls for a vote "by the usual sign," since this confuses the members.

When the chairman is unable to determine on which side the majority voted, he may call for the vote again. If he is still unable to determine the result, he may call for a rising vote on his own initiative.

When he is not certain as to the vote, he may announce, "The Ayes [or Noes] seem to have it" and then hesitate in order to give any member the opportunity to demand a division. If no one responds promptly, the chairman may then say, "The Ayes [or Noes] have it. The motion is carried [or lost]."

If the vote as announced appears to any member to be incorrect, he may call for a division of the assembly in order to verify the vote.[2]

The vote on a motion requiring a two-thirds or three-fourths vote should not be taken by a voice vote but by some method which will give an actual count.

*Rising Vote*

Any member has the right, following the announcement of a voice vote and before any other business intervenes, to "call for a division."[3] A call for a division can interrupt a speaker and does not require a second. It cannot be amended or debated.

When the presiding officer is uncertain as to a voice vote, he may call for a rising vote, and when a division is demanded, he must call for a rising vote. He does this by stating: "Those in favor of the motion, please rise. . . . Be seated. Those opposed, please rise. . . . Be seated. The motion is carried [or lost]."

In small assemblies, or when the vote is close, the members rising should be counted, and they must be counted if a count is demanded by a member and there is any doubt as to the result of the vote. The chairman may count the vote or have the secretary do so. When the count has been taken, the chairman may announce the vote as follows: "The vote is affirmative—48, negative—50. The motion is lost."

Should the chairman prefer, he may verify a voice vote by asking the members to vote by raising their hands. This vote is counted in the same way.

When visitors or others who are not entitled to vote are present and seated with delegates, votes should not be taken by voice but by rising or "by show of hands," in order that voting may be limited to those entitled to vote.

## Voting by Roll Call

Votes should be taken by roll call when it is desired to record the vote of each member. A recorded vote is usually advantageous when members vote as representatives of others. This method is sometimes termed "voting by 'yeas and nays.'" A vote by roll call may be decided upon by majority vote or may be required by the constitution or by-laws. If a vote is to be taken by roll call, the chairman may state the question thus:

"The motion to be voted upon is. . . . Those in favor of the motion will answer 'Yes' as their names are called; those opposed will answer 'No.' The secretary will call the roll."

The names are called in alphabetical order or in the numerical order of districts represented or in some other appropriate order. The name of the presiding officer is called last. If a member does not wish to vote, he may answer "Present." The secretary should always have lists of the names of members arranged in their proper order, ready for use in calling the roll. The original roll-call record is inserted in the minutes.

When the voting is completed, the chairman may announce the vote by saying:

"The vote is: Affirmative—210, Negative—179. The motion is carried."

Or the vote may be more simply announced as:

"Ayes—210, Noes—179. The motion is carried."

The chairman must always take the affirmative vote first and state it first when announcing the vote.

## Voting by Ballot

Voting by ballot is the only method by which members are able to express their decision without revealing their opinions or preferences. This method of voting is usually required in elections and in voting on amendments to the constitution. When a vote by ballot is not required by the constitution or bylaws, it may be ordered by a motion to vote by ballot. This motion requires a majority vote.

When a vote by ballot is required by the constitution or bylaws, any motion to dispense with it or to suspend the provision requiring such a vote is not in order. Such a motion is not in order because it compels a member to reveal his opinion regarding the candidate or proposition. For example, a motion "that the secretary cast a ballot for Mr. A" is not in order. If a member is opposed to Mr. A, he could not vote against this motion without revealing his opposition.

Voting by ballot takes additional time, but it protects the important right of each member to keep his vote secret.

Usually a ballot vote should not be taken when voters are acting in a representative capacity, since those they represent are entitled to know how their delegates vote.

## Method of Balloting

If the candidates or measures to be voted upon are known ahead of voting time, the secretary should have ballots prepared. Printed ballots result in fewer errors than those prepared by members themselves. If prepared ballots are not used, blank slips of paper may be provided on which the members write the names of the candidates whom they favor or the numbers of the propositions.

The presiding officer appoints at least three tellers, one of whom he designates as the chairman, to assist him in taking the vote. The presiding officer should give careful and explicit instructions as to how the members should prepare their ballots.

If blank sheets of paper are used instead of printed ballots, all propositions should be numbered and members should vote for propositions by number. In voting for candidates, both the office and the candidate are written on the ballot. When possible, names of the candidates and numbers of propositions are placed on a blackboard or screen. The presiding officer reads the name of the office and the names of all the candidates for that office. Propositions and their numbers are also read.

It is the tellers' duty to see that each member receives one ballot only, and the presiding officer should ask, before beginning instructions:

"Is anyone without a ballot?"

## Duties of Tellers

It is the duty of the tellers to pass out, collect, and count the ballots and to determine the vote. The tellers should be careful to see that only members entitled to vote do so.

Ballots should be folded to ensure secrecy. The presiding officer directs the tellers where and how to count the ballots. Any member has the right to be present while the ballots are being counted. Even the resignation of the presiding officer who appointed them does not terminate the authority of the tellers to determine and announce the vote.[4]

## Counting Ballots

The following rules are usually observed when counting ballots:

1. When two or more ballots are folded together, they are counted as one illegal vote.

2. Blanks are ignored.

3. Votes for ineligible persons are reported as illegal votes.

4. A technical error, such as spelling, does not invalidate a ballot when the intent of the voter is clear.

5. If the tellers determine that more ballots have been cast than there are legal voters present, the vote must be retaken.

## Tellers' Report of Vote by Ballot

The chairman of tellers, when called upon, reads the report to the assembly without stating whether propositions are carried or candidates are elected and hands it to the presiding officer, who announces which propositions have passed or which candidates are elected. The chairman of the tellers then delivers the ballots to the secretary in a sealed envelope. The secretary preserves these unopened for a reasonable time in case a recount should be ordered by a majority vote.

A tellers' report on a vote by ballot may be as follows:

*Tellers' Report on Propositions I, II, II; Election February 16*

*Proposition I*—To invest surplus funds in United States Bonds

Total vote cast .................................... 423
Illegal votes (three ballots not intelligible) .......... 3
Total legal votes ................................. 420
Number necessary to pass (majority of quorum) ...... 250
Votes for Proposition ............................. 325
Votes against Proposition ......................... 95

*Proposition II*—To authorize sale of clubhouse

Total vote cast .................................... 406
Illegal votes (one altered ballot, two unintelligible) .... 3
Total legal votes ................................. 403
Number necessary to pass ......................... 250
Votes for Proposition ............................. 255
Votes against Proposition ......................... 148

*Proposition III*—To elect officers biennially

Total vote cast .................................... 283
Illegal votes (2 unintelligible, 3 folded together, counted
    as one) ....................................... 3
Total legal votes ................................. 280
Number necessary to pass ......................... 250
Votes for Proposition ............................. 175
Votes against Proposition ......................... 105

All ballots are returned herewith.

(*Signed*) John Smith, *Chairman of Tellers*

## Acting by Unanimous or General Consent

Routine or noncontroversial questions are often decided without taking a formal vote. When members are in substantial agreement, this method of disposing of a question saves time and expedites business. It cannot be used in deciding controversial questions.

When a matter of routine business comes up for consideration, it is the usual practice in many organizations for a member, instead of making a motion, to ask "unanimous consent" to do a certain thing. He may, for example, request unanimous consent to have the committee on credentials report immediately. The presiding officer may respond:

"If there is no objection, the committee will report immediately."

The presiding officer should hesitate for an instant to give an opportunity for objection, and if there is no objection, he directs the chairman of the committee to present the report.

It is a well-established practice in many organizations to act by unanimous consent on some matters coming up under the regular order of business. The most usual is the approval of the minutes. After the minutes are read (and, if necessary, corrected), the chairman, without waiting for a motion, may say:

"If there is no objection, the minutes will be approved as read [or, as corrected]."

If there is objection to a request for unanimous consent, it is necessary that the question be presented as a motion and that the motion be put to vote in the usual way.

Actions by unanimous consent may be initiated by the presiding officer. He may, without waiting for a motion, proceed by assuming "unanimous consent." For example, if a member asks leave to make an announcement at a time different from that provided in the regular order of business for announcements, the presiding officer may say:

"If there is no objection, Mr. M will be allowed to make an announcement at this time."

If, upon a request for unanimous consent, any member says, "I object," procedure by unanimous consent must be abandoned. Even if the presiding officer has announced that an action is taken by unanimous consent and any member immediately says, "I object," the question must be stated by the presiding officer and voted upon in the regular manner.

The tactful presiding officer, who is responsive to the

wishes of the assembly, senses when matters may be transacted by informal consideration and by unanimous consent and recognizes the time when every technicality must be observed.

## Voting by Mail

In organizations whose members are scattered through a state or country or throughout the world, arrangements are often made to allow members to vote on important questions by mail. These frequently include amendments to the constitution and bylaws and election of officers. In order to vote by mail this method of voting must be provided for in the bylaws unless authorized by the charter of the organization.

Any method of voting by mail which makes the questions to be voted upon clear may be followed unless the bylaws provide for a particular plan. A copy of the proposed amendments or measures or a list of the candidates may be mailed to each member by the secretary, together with directions for marking the ballot.

The ballots must be marked and returned to the secretary within a specified time. One way to ensure secrecy is to require each member to seal his ballot in one envelope with no mark of identification and to enclose it in another envelope bearing his signature or some other identification. The secretary checks the signatures on the outer envelopes against the signatures of those entitled to vote and delivers the inner envelopes containing the ballots, still sealed, to the tellers. To give members information concerning measures or candidates to be voted upon, provision may be made for the leaders of both sides to enclose their arguments with the ballots.

## Voting by Proxy

Voting by proxy is a method by which one person casts a

vote in the place of, and by the permission or request of, an absent member. Voting by proxy means that a person who is entitled to vote assigns in writing his right to vote to another member, who then is entitled to cast as many votes as he holds proxies. In corporation meetings where membership is based upon the possession of stock, voting by proxy is usually permitted by law. The use of proxies in organizations where all members have an equal right in voting is ill-advised and is never permissible unless specifically authorized by the bylaws.

## Changing a Vote

A member may change his vote only up to the time that the vote is finally announced. This rule is necessary to give finality to a vote. Any supposed right of a member to change his vote, even by unanimous consent, after the vote has been finally announced, is a misinterpretation of parliamentary law. After a vote has been announced a member can change the record of his vote only upon clear proof that an error was made in recording it. When voting by ballot a member may not change his vote after the ballot has been deposited in the ballot box.

## Determination of the Result of a Vote

It is the duty of the presiding officer to announce the result of a vote according to the facts.[5] However, an untrue or incorrect announcement of a vote by the presiding officer cannot make the vote, as cast by the majority, illegal.[6] In case of a disputed vote, the courts will examine the facts to determine whether the vote as announced is correct.[7]

# Chapter 11. NOMINATIONS AND ELECTIONS

## Time of Holding Elections

The regular time of holding elections for officers is determined by the constitution or bylaws. Elections to fill vacancies or to select delegates or committees may be held at any regular meeting or at a special meeting called for that purpose, if no contradictory provision is included in the bylaws.

## Determining Methods of Nominating and Voting

A nomination is the formal presentation to the assembly of the name of a candidate for the office to be filled. It may be made from the floor by a member or it may be proposed in a report of a nominating committee.

If no method of nominating and voting upon candidates is provided for in the constitution or bylaws of the organization, any member may present a motion determining the method. If an election is pending, this motion is an incidental motion. The motion may be amended but can have no other motions applied to it.

## Nominations from the Floor

Nominations from the floor are in order as soon as the chairman calls for them. The chairman may say:

"Nominations for the office of president are now in order."

Any member may rise and nominate another member as follows:

"I nominate Mr. Y for president."

A nomination does not require a second, although seconds may be permitted if some member desires to express his approval of a candidate. It is customary to preface the nomination by a speech describing the fitness of the candidate. If the assembly does not object, this proceeding is permissible. In very large organizations nominating speeches are valuable to acquaint the members with the candidate and his qualifications. In small assemblies where the candidates are known to all members, nominating speeches serve little purpose.

As a chairman hears a name placed in nomination, he repeats it, and the secretary records it while another member may place the name on a blackboard or screen. No member may nominate more than one candidate for each office while other members desire to nominate candidates.

## Nominations by Nominating Committee

The other method of nomination is by a nominating committee whose duty it is to select and present the names of the nominees. This committee may be elected as provided in the bylaws, or if these contain no provision for the selection of a nominating committee, the assembly may choose its own method. It is best that the president have no part in selecting the nominating committee and he should not serve on it, even as a member ex officio. Usually the committee is chosen at the meeting preceding the election or at an earlier meeting in order that ample time may be allowed to select candidates. The nominating committee submits its report at the time named in its instructions or at the time provided in the bylaws. This report to the organization presents the names of one or more members as candidates for each office to be filled.

This method of nomination by a committee has several advantages. It is possible to interview prospective nominees and to make sure that they will accept the nomination and serve if elected. A more thorough investigation of the nominee's qualifications is possible. The committee can also apportion representation among different groups more equitably.

When the report of the nominating committee is presented, the persons named in the report are considered nominated just as though they had been nominated from the floor. The chairman asks if there are any further nominations for each office separately and in turn, and if there are any nominations made from the floor, these are added to the list of nominees presented by the committee.

## Closing Nominations

When there appear to be no further nominations, the chairman inquires:

"Are there any further nominations for the office of president?"

If no other nominations are presented, the chairman may call for nominations for the next office, or some member may propose a motion to close nominations. This motion requires only a majority vote. Some writers on parliamentary procedure have been confused concerning the vote required to close nominations. This motion cannot be proposed until a reasonable time has been given for the presentation of additional names. No motion to close nominations is necessary, and the election may begin as soon as there are no further nominations. The motion to close nominations usually serves no useful purpose because the members can vote for anyone they desire, regardless of whether his name was placed in nomination.

When nominations have been formally closed, but voting has not begun, they may be reopened by a motion to this effect. This motion requires a majority vote.

## Voting for Candidates Not Nominated

Regardless of how nominations are made, members are not limited to voting for the candidates nominated. Except when voting viva voce, they may vote for anyone who is eligible, regardless of whether he has been nominated, and anyone receiving the necessary vote is elected.

It is not uncommon to combine the nomination and election when voting by ballot. There being no formal nominations, members may vote for any eligible member.

## Voting on Candidates

After the nominations are closed, the assembly proceeds to vote upon the names of candidates by the method laid down in the constitution or bylaws or determined by motion. If the constitution or bylaws make no provision for voting, it may be done by any of the methods which the assembly may choose.

Irregularities in an election which do not affect the result do not invalidate an election,[1] but substantial violation of the rules does invalidate an election.[2]

When the election is to be by voice or rising vote, a vote may be taken on each office as soon as the candidates for that particular office have been nominated, or it may be delayed until nominations for all offices have been made. When the election is by ballot, nominations for all offices are completed before the balloting and one ballot may be used for all offices.

## Vote Necessary to Elect

The vote necessary to elect is usually fixed in the constitution or bylaws. Unless otherwise provided, the following rules govern:

1. When a candidate receives a majority of the legal votes cast, he is elected.
2. A candidate who receives a plurality of all the legal votes cast, or more than any other candidate, is not elected in the absence of a provision to that effect in the constitution or bylaws or standing rules.
3. When a majority vote is required and no candidate receives a majority, the vote must be retaken.

## Proportional Voting

Some organizations require that when no candidate receives a majority vote, the next vote is taken on only the two candidates who received the highest vote. Others provide that the candidate with the lowest vote be dropped as each successive vote is taken. Some organizations provide for proportional voting. A simple proportional voting system, often used where two or more offices of the same rank are to be filled, is to allow each voter as many votes as there are candidates to be elected and to permit the voters to distribute their votes or cumulate them upon one candidate. The usual effect of proportional voting is to ensure representation of important minority groups.

## Casting a Ballot

When there is only one candidate for an office, some member occasionally moves that the secretary cast a ballot to elect the candidate. This practice of declaring an officer elected as the result of a cast ballot cannot be substituted for a vote by ballot since some other member, not nominated, may be elected if a general vote is taken by ballot.[3]

## Motion to Make a Vote Unanimous

A unanimous vote means all the legal votes cast. One common error is to suppose that a vote can be made unanimous by a motion to that effect. In elections only the candidate receiving the second highest number of votes or one of his friends should propose a motion to make a vote unanimous. This motion has no legal effect. The motion to make a vote unanimous, though intended as a complimentary gesture, does not change the legal vote in any particular, much less make it unanimous.

## When Elections Become Effective

An election becomes effective immediately if the candidate is present and does not decline or if he is absent and has consented to his candidacy. If he is absent and has not consented to his nomination, the election becomes effective as soon as he is notified, if he does not decline immediately. Unless some other time is specified in the bylaws, an officer assumes his office as soon as he has been elected. Often the bylaws provide for the installation of officers at a future meeting.

# PART II
## ORGANIZATIONS—THEIR STRUCTURE AND FUNCTIONS

# Chapter 12. SETTING UP A NEW
## ORGANIZATION

### Temporary and Permanent Organizations

Organizations may be divided into two types according to the probable length of their existence. These are temporary organizations and permanent organizations. A temporary organization is one existing for a few meetings or even a single meeting. It dissolves automatically as soon as the purpose for which it is formed is accomplished. Examples of temporary organizations are a mass meeting, an organization to elect a particular candidate to office, and an organization to secure the passage or repeal of a certain law. A permanent organization is one formed with the intention of functioning over a considerable period of time or indefinitely.

### Preliminary Plans for Establishing an Organization

Since it is very difficult to formulate plans in a large assembly, the founders of either a temporary or a permanent organization should meet in a small group or committee and make the necessary preliminary decisions. Among more important preliminary questions to be decided are the following:

1. What is the purpose of the proposed organization?
2. How can this purpose be explained and made clear at the organization meeting?
3. How is the purpose to be accomplished?
4. How is the organization to be financed?
5. Who is to be admitted to membership?
6. Is there to be more than one type of membership?
7. How are the members to be selected?
8. What are the policies of the new organization and how are they to be determined?
9. What is to be its relationship to other organizations?
10. Is it to be affiliated with an already established national organization? If so, help and suggestions for setting up the initial organization, as well as the requirements for national membership, can be secured from the national headquarters before the first meeting.
11. Who are to be the temporary officers?
12. Is the organization to be incorporated?

## Plans for First Meeting

When the committee or group of founders has agreed upon the answer to these general questions, it decides upon plans for the initial meeting. Among the problems to be decided concerning the first meeting are the following:

1. What is to be the type of the initial meeting—mass meeting, dinner, or general meeting?
2. When and where is the first meeting to be held?
3. How are the proposed members to be called together —by telephone, letter, press, or radio?
4. Who is to call the meeting to order?
5. Who is to be nominated for chairman?
6. Who is to nominate the chairman?
7. Who is to explain the purpose of the meeting?

8. Who is to write the resolutions or bylaws to be voted on?

When these questions are satisfactorily answered, it is time to draw up a resolution establishing the group as an organization, and if the organization is to be a permanent one, to draft a set of bylaws. When all this preliminary work has been done, the founders are ready to call the first meeting.

## The First Meeting of an Organization

When the group which has been invited to the initial meeting comes together, a member previously selected should rise and call the meeting to order [1] thus:

"The meeting will please come to order. I nominate Mr. A for temporary chairman."

The member who calls the meeting to order may ask for nominations from the floor instead of making the nomination himself. The vote on the nomination is taken thus:

"Those in favor of Mr. A for temporary chairman say, 'Aye.' . . . Those opposed, 'No.' . . ."

The chairman announces the result as follows:

"A majority having voted for Mr. A, he is elected temporary chairman. Mr. A will please take the chair."

Usually only one person is nominated for temporary chairman, but if additional persons are nominated, a vote is taken on each name, in the order of their nomination, until one candidate receives a majority. This candidate is then declared elected and becomes the presiding officer. The presiding officer then opens nominations for a temporary secretary, who is selected in the same manner as the temporary chairman.

After the temporary secretary has been elected, the chairman calls upon one or more of the prospective members to explain the purpose of the meeting. Some member should present the previously phrased motion or resolution that the assembly form itself into an organization. The following is an example of a resolution setting up a temporary organization:

*Resolved,* That this assembly form itself into a temporary organization for the purpose of protesting against the proposed action of the County Board of Supervisors in granting a franchise to the Ocean Railway Company; and be it further

*Resolved,* That the temporary chairman and a committee of this meeting attend the next meeting of the County Board of Supervisors as representatives of this organization, and that they present to the board a signed protest against the granting of the franchise; and be it further

*Resolved,* That a copy of these resolutions, with a list of the names of all members present and a summary of the principal speeches made at this meeting be sent to each newspaper published in this county.

## Permanent Organizations

A decision to form a permanent organization may be embodied in a resolution or in a motion such as:

"I move that this assembly form a permanent organization to be known as the Piedmont Chamber of Commerce."

If this motion or resolution receives a majority vote, some member moves to appoint a committee to draft a constitution and bylaws, or if a committee has previously drafted these, it is asked to report. When the constitution or the bylaws are presented they are read as a whole, and then each article or section is read separately and discussed, and may be amended. Then the constitution or bylaws are adopted as a whole. As soon as the bylaws have been adopted, permanent officers may be elected; and with the election of such officers the organization is complete.

The form of constitution and bylaws is discussed in Chapter 14.

## Chapter 13. LAWS GOVERNING

## ORGANIZATIONS

### Kinds of Organizations

The terms "organization" and "assembly," in the broad sense, apply to all groups of persons that are organized and that have officers and rules. These include associations, clubs, societies, lodges, unions, and similar groups. From a legal standpoint organizations are divided into two main groups, incorporated and unincorporated organizations.

### Incorporated Organizations

There is a clear distinction between incorporated and unincorporated organizations. An incorporated organization has a charter and possesses certain authority as an entity, which is separate from its members. Its charter is granted by a sovereign authority, usually the state. Incorporated organizations are required to conform to the laws governing corporations and are subject, to a considerable extent, to regulation by law.

Because of the rather strict regulation of corporations, and because there is considerable variation between the laws of the individual states, an attorney should always be consulted about the details of organizing an incorporated association.

## Advantages of Incorporation

The laws governing incorporated organizations guarantee to the members a definite protection of their interests in the organization. Each member is in a position to insist that the affairs of the organization be conducted according to the law. Incorporated organizations are required to keep records, and any member has the right to inspect these records and can readily compel an accounting of the funds.

The greatest advantage of incorporation is that the members of the corporation are protected from personal liability for the debts of the organization. A corporation is liable for its contracts, for the acts of its officers and agents, and for damages resulting from their negligence, but the members are afforded general protection from personal liability in such instances.

## Unincorporated Organizations

An unincorporated organization or association has much greater freedom to operate without regard to technical provisions of law, but in several important respects the members are not so well protected. Since the organization is not a separate legal entity, the law imposes responsibility directly upon the members, and any member may be held personally responsible for all of the debts of the organization.

A person who is invited to join an unincorporated organization should investigate the financial status and responsibility of the organization very carefully before becoming a member. Court decisions are proof of the fact that many persons have joined what purported to be a purely friendly and social country club or athletic association only to find that their personal properties and savings could be taken from them to pay the debts of the club.

The responsibilities and liabilities of a member of an unincorporated organization are similar to the responsibilities and liabilities of a member of a partnership. The members of an unincorporated organization conducted for profit are generally held to be partners.[1]

## Liability of Unincorporated Organizations under Special Statutes

In addition to the general laws governing the operations of unincorporated organizations, there are special statutes passed by the state and Federal governments which also control them.

The courts have upheld statutes permitting suits against organizations for any cause of action, upon which a person could maintain a suit against members of the association.[2] The courts have also held that jurisdiction may be acquired over an association by service of process upon one or more of its members,[3] or upon specified officers of the association,[4] and that an action may be maintained against an association in its common or association name.[5] The property of individual members is liable for satisfaction of a judgment against the organization.[6] Only the members of an unincorporated organization are liable, unless a special statute places liability on others.[7]

## Powers of Unincorporated Organizations

Every organization is limited to those powers which can be exercised in compliance with law, and any illegal act is beyond its power.[8]

Ordinarily, the constitution, bylaws, or charter of an organization determines its powers.[9] An organization with a charter, constitution, or bylaws can perform any legal act within the purpose for which it was formed.[10] The powers of all organizations are governed to a considerable extent by the common law, and they are also governed by the appropriate parliamentary law in all matters not covered by statute, charter, constitution, bylaws, or rules.[11]

The rules of parliamentary law applicable to a particular organization can be modified by setting forth in the bylaws or rules of the organization the desired variations from parliamentary law.[12] Since there is not complete agreement between parliamentary authorities, it is advantageous to adopt a particular manual to guide the organization on all matters not governed by statute, bylaws, or rules. When a particular manual is adopted, the organization is governed by that manual.[13]

When not otherwise determined, the powers of an organization can be ascertained from the established practices or usages acquiesced in by the members.[14]

### Inherent Powers and Responsibilities of Unincorporated Organizations

In the absence of a special statute authorizing it, an association cannot hold real property in its own name,[15] but it can hold or dispose of money or other personal property.[16] This ability arises from the importance given in law to the possession of personal property and to the right of anyone to use or dispose of personal property in his possession unless some other person can establish a better right to it. Trustees can hold property, either real or personal, for the benefit of an unincorporated organization. An unincorporated organization can, by majority vote, expend its funds to carry out its purposes, but it can expend money for no other purpose without the consent of all of its members.[17]

An unincorporated organization has no general authority to enter into contracts, but contracts made in its name by its officers or members are enforceable against the officers and members and against third parties.[18]

An unincorporated organization is responsible for the wrongful acts of its officers and members, who are engaged in carrying out the business of the organization. It may also be held liable when their acts have been ratified by the association.[19] An association cannot commit a crime, but its officers or members may be convicted of crimes for acts committed on behalf of the organization.[20]

## Dissolution of Organizations

An organization may be dissolved by the following:

1. Surrender of its charter to a superior authority.[21]
2. Death or withdrawal of members. An organization is not dissolved so long as enough members remain to carry on the purposes of the organization.[22]
3. Incorporation of an unincorporated organization, since an inherently new organization comes into being.[23]
4. Abandonment. Mere failure to hold meetings or elect officers does not necessarily constitute abandonment.
5. Consent of members. A minority may keep an organization after a majority has voted to dissolve.[24]
6. Consolidation with other organizations.[25]
7. Reorganization, when the new organization differs substantially from the old and is in effect a new organization.[26]

# Chapter 14. CONSTITUTION, BYLAWS, AND

## STANDING RULES

*Rules Governing Organizations*

An organization may be governed by statutes, a charter, a constitution, bylaws, or standing rules or by two or more of these. If the organization is incorporated, the primary rules under which it operates are the incorporation laws of the state under which it is incorporated. Next in rank are the rules included in its charter or constitution. Following in rank are the bylaws and standing rules. In all matters not covered by the charter, constitution, bylaws, or standing rules, the parliamentary authority adopted by the organization controls.

Organizations which are not incorporated operate under any general laws which are applicable and under their constitution as the next highest source of law.[1] Next in rank are the bylaws. Many organizations prefer to consolidate in one document the provisions usually contained in the constitution and in the bylaws, and the document is usually called "bylaws" or "constitution and bylaws." This plan is desirable since it is simpler and avoids confusion. Rules relating to procedure peculiar to the organization are sometimes included in a group of rules known as "standing rules." In all situations not covered by these groups of rules, the parliamentary authority adopted by the organization governs.

## Adopting Parliamentary Authority

Every deliberative organization is presumed by law to be governed by the rules of parliamentary law. The charter, constitution, bylaws, and standing rules of the organization are its highest authority; but in all matters not covered by these rules the organization is governed by parliamentary law.

An organization can adopt any code or book of rules on parliamentary procedure to govern it, and the name of the authority should be included in the bylaws or standing rules. This bylaw is usually stated in a form similar to the following:

"In all matters not covered by its constitution and bylaws this organization shall be governed by the *Sturgis Standard Code of Parliamentary Procedure.*"

Great care should be given to the selection of a parliamentary authority because the courts do not excuse any organization from its legal requirements because of errors or omissions or ambiguities in the authority which may have been adopted. Ignorance of the correct rules of procedure is not a valid defense against legal entanglements or action.

## Function of Constitution and Bylaws

The function of the constitution or of the bylaws of an organization is to define the privileges secured and the duties assumed by the members [2] and to set up the framework of the organization. An organization has the right to adopt such constitution and bylaws as the members may agree upon, so long as they are not contrary to public policy or to the law.[3]

A constitution is a compilation of the fundamental rules defining the government of an organization.[4] Any rule in the bylaws, standing rules, or in general parliamentary procedure which conflicts with the constitution is invalid, insofar as the particular organization is concerned.

The bylaws may include the provisions sometimes found in a constitution and also more specific regulations for the conduct of the organization. They are usually more detailed than the constitution.

## Drafting a Constitution

The first duty of a committee appointed to draft a constitution and bylaws is to make certain that the committee members understand thoroughly the purposes and the plans for the proposed organization. These purposes may be made more concrete by detailed discussion among the committee members and by consulting persons outside the committee who are interested in the proposed organization.

The next step should be a survey of the constitutions and the bylaws which have worked well for similar organizations. Collections of constitutions and bylaws of successful organizations are available in most libraries. These collections contain comments on the advantages or disadvantages of the different provisions.

Once the purposes of the proposed organization are determined and the type of constitution and the bylaws decided upon, the actual writing of the constitution and the bylaws is not a difficult task.

## Articles of a Constitution

A constitution consists of a few fundamental provisions which should be set forth with brevity and clarity. There are at least seven provisions which are usually stated in separate articles. Each article may be divided into sections. The various articles and the subjects which each covers are as follows:

*Article I* states the name of the organization.

*Article II* states the purposes and powers of the organization.

*Article III* states the qualifications of members. It may limit the number of members or contain other provisions relating to members.

*Article IV* contains a list of the officers of the organization and states their duties and the length of their term of office.

*Article V* provides for a board of directors or governing board or an executive committee and for the method of selecting it. If no board is desired, this article is omitted.

*Article VI* states the time for regular meetings and provides a method by which special meetings may be called.

*Article VII* contains a statement of the method of amending the constitution and of the vote required for amendments.

A preamble may preface the constitution and usually contains the reasons for the formation of the organization.

*Drafting Bylaws*

The bylaws contain all of the details necessary to amplify and carry out the provisions of the constitution. All bylaws dealing with the same general subject are grouped together under one article, which in turn is divided into sections. For instance, there are usually several bylaws or provisions relating to committees, each of which constitutes a section. These sections should be arranged in consecutive order, and together they form a bylaw or article entitled "Committees."

## Provisions of Bylaws

When an organization dispenses with a constitution, all of the subjects which would otherwise be covered by a constitution are included in the bylaws, and it is possible to group all important rules dealing with one subject under a single heading. In addition to the usual constitutional provisions, bylaws ordinarily include the following:

1. Kinds of membership
2. Detailed requirements for membership
3. Method of admitting members
4. Dues
5. Powers and duties of officers
6. Powers and duties of committees
7. Election of officers and committees, including the vote required for election
8. Provisions for calling and conducting meetings
9. Parliamentary authority
10. Number constituting a quorum
11. Vote required for important decisions
12. Procedure for amending bylaws

## Adoption of a Constitution and Bylaws

When the committee appointed to draft a constitution and bylaws is ready to report, the chairman presents the report and recommendations of the committee and moves that the constitution be adopted. The presiding officer may state the motion in the following form:

"It has been moved and seconded that the constitution be adopted. The constitution will now be read."

The chairman of the committee either reads the constitution as a whole or hands it to the secretary to read. Then each article and section is read separately, and as soon as each is read, the chairman calls for amendments and discussion. If an amendment is proposed, the chairman states this to the assembly, and after discussion it is voted upon, but no article or section itself is voted upon at this time. When the reading and amending of all the articles and sections of the constitution is completed, the chairman asks:

"Are there any amendments to the constitution as a whole, or is there any further discussion?"

When any amendments proposed have been disposed of and no one rises to discuss the constitution further, the chairman takes the vote upon the motion to adopt the constitution. A majority vote is sufficient for its adoption. Following this vote, if there are separate bylaws they are read, considered, and amended individually, and voted upon as a whole in the same manner as the constitution.

## When the Constitution and Bylaws Go into Effect

The constitution or bylaws, or both, go into effect immediately after the announcement of the vote adopting them. If it is desired that some portion of the constitution or bylaws shall not go into effect until a later date, this reservation should be included in the motion to adopt. If not included in the original motion, such reservations may be added as amendments to the motion to adopt or they may be made as separate motions. In either case, a majority vote is required. The following is an example of a motion to adopt a constitution with reservations:

"I move that the constitution be adopted as last read, except that Section 4 of Article III, which establishes a method by which nonmembers may be admitted to associate membership, shall not go into effect until after the next meeting."

## Amendment of Constitution and Bylaws

Constitutions and bylaws provide within themselves a method by which they may be amended. Two requirements are usually included in this provision. The first requirement is that notice be given at one or more meetings immediately preceding the one at which the amendment is to be voted upon. The second requirement is a statement of the vote necessary to adopt amendments.

## Notice of Amendments

A constitution or bylaws should state explicitly what kind of notice is required for the adoption of amendments. These provisions vary widely. Some organizations provide only that notice must be given at a previous meeting or meetings. Others require that notice be given and that the amendment be read and submitted in writing to the secretary at a preceding meeting. Other organizations require that the proposed amendment be sent to each member in printed form, with the notice of the meeting. The essence of a provision for previous notice is that each member must know what the proposed amendment is and when it is to be voted upon.

When the time specified in the notice arrives, the organization must confine itself strictly to the consideration of the amendments as they were stated in the notice. Except when the exact text of the amendments is required to be set out in full in the notice, any amendments which are germane to the subject are in order, but no new subject not specified may be introduced. No amendment to any other portion of a constitution or bylaws, not mentioned in the notice, is in order.

## Vote Required for Amendments

The second requirement that must be included in the provision for amending a constitution is that the proposed amendment must secure the affirmative vote of a definite percentage of the members. Usually a two-thirds or three-fourths vote of the members voting at a meeting, a quorum being present, is required. In small organizations this requirement often reads, "a two-thirds vote of the total membership," but such a requirement would make it almost impossible for a large organization to amend its constitution.

The exact vote required for amendment of both the constitution and bylaws must be specified. If an organization has bylaws only, rules for their amendment should be the same as for amendments to constitutions. If an organization operates under both constitution and bylaws, it should be possible to amend a bylaw with somewhat more ease and rapidity than is permitted in amending a constitution.

## Revision of Constitution and Bylaws

After constitutions and bylaws have served for a period of time, it is often necessary to amend several portions of them. The simplest method, when extensive changes are to be made, is to select a Committee on Revision of the Constitution and Bylaws, whose duty it is to study the constitution and bylaws in detail and submit a report of suggested amendments. An entirely new constitution or bylaws may be suggested as an amendment, or only a few changes may be recommended.

The report of the committee, when read, is equivalent to giving notice of proposed amendments. The report cannot be acted upon until the time required for notice has elapsed. When the time for decision on the amendments arrives, each proposed change is considered and voted upon separately, unless a new constitution has been submitted, in which case the rules for adopting a new constitution are followed.

## Standing Rules

Organizations have a right to create standing rules by majority vote without notice, and to abolish them in the same manner. Standing rules cover points of lesser importance than those contained in constitutions or bylaws. Any rules of procedure which an organization desires and which vary from the general rules of parliamentary procedure or the adopted parliamentary authority may be included in the standing rules.

The following are examples of subjects commonly included in standing rules:

1. Limitations on length of speeches
2. Order of business
3. Hour of meeting
4. Fines for minor infractions
5. Regulations concerning guests at meetings
6. Special assessments
7. Entertainment of guest speakers

When no separate standing rules are adopted, these provisions are usually included in the bylaws.

## Chapter 15. MINUTES

### How Minutes Are Taken

Unless an organization provides for a verbatim report of meetings taken by a reporter, the secretary takes notes which are sufficiently complete and accurate so that he can prepare the minutes correctly. The secretary should not attempt to take minutes in final form at the meeting.

When the minutes are completed, they are written in or inserted in the official minutes book and signed by the secretary. The minutes book remains in the custody of the secretary or the recording secretary at all times, but it is open to the inspection of any member.

### What Minutes Contain

Minutes contain a record of all proceedings, but, except in those organizations which take minutes verbatim, no record of discussions. Minutes are a record of things done, of business introduced, of reports made, and of votes taken. All motions, whether passed or lost, are recorded with the name of the proposer. It is also good practice to record the name of the seconder. When a vote is taken by roll call, by ballot, or by division which is counted, the number voting on each side is recorded. When a vote is taken by roll call, the record of each member's vote is put in the minutes.

Reports of officers and committees may be summarized briefly or mentioned as having been presented. In either case, a copy of the report is filed in the committee report book, and the page number is included in the minutes.

Minutes of hearings or other special types of meetings should be more complete and detailed. Minutes of committee hearings should list all persons who speak for or against questions, and often give a summary of the arguments. A committee or its chairman may, in special instances, require the minutes to be taken in a particular manner.

## What Minutes Should Not Contain

*62693*

Under no circumstances does the secretary include his personal opinions or interpretations. In some organizations it is still customary to use descriptive words in the minutes, such as "a brilliant suggestion," "very heated discussion," "an able report," or "a pertinent speech." These phrases are out of place in minutes. Tributes to members should appear as votes of thanks or resolutions of gratitude. The secretary is a recorder of transactions, not a reporter or interpreter of sentiment.

## Form of Minutes

The minutes of organizations vary greatly according to their particular needs, but there is an opening form which most organizations follow. The first sentence contains the following facts:

1. The name of the organization
2. The kind of meeting (regular, special, adjourned)
3. The time, place, and date when the meeting was called to order
4. The name of the presiding officer

The body of the minutes is made up of a brief chronological record of actions taken or business transacted. Motions are recorded in a form such as "Mr. B moved that the annual tournament be held on June sixth. Seconded by Mr. M. Motion carried." The record of committee reports might be made as follows:

"Mr. D, chairman of the Committee on Finance, presented his annual report. See page 623, *Committee Report Book*."

## How Minutes Are Corrected and Approved

The presiding officer calls upon the secretary to read the minutes at the proper place in the order of business. If a member moves that the reading of the minutes be postponed or dispensed with, this may be arranged by majority vote.

At the conclusion of the reading of the minutes, the presiding officer calls for corrections.

He may say:

"Are there any corrections to the minutes?"

He then pauses for a moment. If no additions or corrections are suggested, he may then say:

"There being no corrections, the minutes will be [or stand] approved as read."

When corrections are suggested, they are usually made by unanimous consent. The presiding officer may say:

"If there is no objection, the error pointed out by Mr. A will be corrected."

If there is disagreement as to the correctness of the minutes or as to the proposed correction, the presiding officer, without waiting for a motion, may put the question to vote. If the question is on the correctness of the minutes, he may put the question to vote by saying:

"Those who consider the minutes correct as read say, 'Aye.' . . . Those opposed say, 'No.'"

Or if the question is on a proposed correction, the question may be put as:

"Those in favor of making the correction as proposed by Mr. B say, 'Aye.' . . . Those opposed say, 'No.'"

After all corrections have been made, some member may move to approve the minutes as corrected, or the chairman may state:

"If there are no further corrections, the minutes will be approved as corrected."

When the minutes have been approved, the secretary writes the word "Approved" and the date of the approval at the close of the minutes and signs his name.

It is a practice of many organizations to send copies of the minutes to all members as soon as they can be prepared following the meetings. This keeps all of the members advised concerning the business conducted by their organization and gives those who attended the opportunity to point out errors in the minutes.

## Minutes Committee

In order to save the time spent in reading and correcting the minutes, there is a growing trend among larger organizations to provide for the reading and correction of minutes by a minutes committee. A committee is selected, which is responsible for reading, correcting, and approving the minutes in the same way that an auditing committee approves financial records and certifies to their correctness.

If an organization does not wish to hear the minutes read, it is important to have a standing committee on minutes to which all minutes are referred for correction and approval.

## Duties of Minutes Committee

When a minutes committee has the responsibility for reading, correcting, and certifying its approval of the minutes, at least two of the members should take notes of proceedings to serve as a check on the secretary's record. A minutes committee submits a brief report at least annually.

Organizations should not make a practice of deferring, postponing, or dispensing with the reading of the minutes. The lapse of time promotes mistakes through forgetfulness. When minutes are not regularly read at the following meeting, they are best handled by reference to a minutes committee. The reading of minutes should never be dispensed with unless provision for checking and correction is made.

The minutes committee is of particular value when minutes are to be printed, because it acts as an additional safeguard against errors in the record.

# Chapter 16. THE PRESIDING OFFICER AND
## HIS DUTIES

## The Presiding Officer as a Leader

The president, or the head of an organization whatever his title may be, should be chosen for two qualifications. These are his ability to lead and his ability to preside. As a leader, an understanding and an appreciation of human nature is one of his most important qualifications. Parliamentary procedure provides the legal and technical machinery for determining the will of the majority, but the carrying out of the majority will is a problem of human collaboration, which the president must direct.

An organization is not merely a group of people working toward some financial, social, or cultural aim. It is also a human organization, through which men and women are trying to express their individual hopes and aims and aspirations. A real leader keeps the fundamental aim of the group always in mind and forges ahead toward that collective goal, but he is not blind to the individual human goals. Except in a great emergency, no good leader presses toward a group goal with such efficiency that he sacrifices individual human relationships and human hopes.

Skill in handling people comes from recognition of the fact that sentiments and reactions to sentiments are important influences in welding people together or in dividing them. The experienced president understands that logic, argument, and facts must be tempered by a consideration for human sentiments, prejudices, and traditions. This human understanding is one of the most important factors of leadership.

## The President as a Presiding Officer

A president's success as a presiding officer depends upon his ability to remain impartial and to keep business moving steadily ahead. The presiding officer acts as a judge, not as a partisan advocate. Any tinge of partisanship or favoritism will soon destroy the respect of members for their president. The presiding officer's duty is to carry out the will of the assembly and not to force or coerce the assembly into carrying out his will, the will of any group or faction, or even the will of the assembly as he personally interprets it.

Presiding is an art which no book of rules can fully teach. The tactful chairman knows how to discourage courteously the member who talks too much or too often, and how to encourage the shy member who speaks only when impelled by strong convictions. He knows, when an assembly is restive, how to shorten discussion and when to make business move along.

Above all things, he knows parliamentary law and how to apply it. It is the president's duty to see that all of the members understand any technical terms of parliamentary procedure which are used in the meeting. The technical language of parliamentary law is often not comprehensible to beginners. The president should serve as interpreter. A poised, courteous chairman uses parliamentary procedure to help the members carry out their desires. A chairman should never rule a bewildered member out of order without courteously explaining why, and if the member's proposal is not in order then, without explaining to him how and when he may accomplish his purpose.

## Decorum in Presiding

The presiding officer, whether he is known as chairman, president, commander, moderator, or by some other title, is always addressed by his official title. If one does not know the title of the presiding officer, he is addressed as "Mr. Chairman" or if a woman, as "Madam Chairman."

The presiding officer observes certain matters of decorum:

1. He stands whenever he is addressing the assembly or a member and is seated only during longer speeches.
2. An efficient chairman keeps the assembly in order at all times. He uses his gavel, which is his symbol of authority, very sparingly. He is alert to the indications of inattention and acts to restore strict order at the first sign of disturbance or disorder. A firm refusal to recognize any member or to entertain any business until order is restored will usually quiet an assembly. A presiding officer who has to resort to frequent gavel pounding is inefficient.
3. The presiding officer refers to himself by his title as "the chair" or "the chairman." He may say "the chair requests" or "the chairman rules." "The chair" is an impartial, impersonal head, and is the "first servant of the assembly" as well as its leader.

## Duties of the Presiding Officer

The usual duties of the presiding officer are as follows:

1. He calls the meeting to order at the appointed time.
2. He announces the business which should come before the assembly in its proper order.
3. He assigns the floor to members who desire to speak.

Once he has recognized the right of a member to the floor, it is the duty of the presiding officer to protect the speaker from disturbance or interference. On the other hand, the presiding officer must never hesitate, when the interest of the organization or its members requires, to permit a speaker to be interrupted.

4. He states all motions that have been correctly proposed and seconded and restates, in the best possible form and without changing the meaning, any motion the proposer has failed to state correctly or clearly. Any restatement or change must be acceptable, however, to the proposer.

5. He explains what the effect of a motion would be if it is not clear to every member. He makes certain that members understand exactly what business is pending.

6. He restricts discussion to the question before the assembly.

7. He answers all parliamentary inquiries and decides points of order and questions of privilege as soon as they arise, but never discusses a motion from the chair.

8. When discussion on a question has ceased or has been closed by a motion to that effect, the presiding officer restates the exact question upon which the assembly is to vote and puts the question to vote.

9. He votes in case of a tie when authorized by the by-laws.

10. He states definitely and clearly the vote and the result of the vote.

11. He protects the assembly from annoyance by refusing to recognize motions that are frivolous in character or that are made solely for the purpose of blocking business or of consuming time.

12. He signs all acts or orders necessary to carry out the will of the assembly.

13. He acts as the representative of the organization to outside persons or to other organized bodies whenever necessary.

In many organizations the presiding officer has additional duties. Some organizations require their presiding officer to act as ex-officio member of committees, to appoint committees, to fill vacancies, or to act as an executive officer. These are not duties that parliamentary law requires of every presiding officer. Therefore, if an organization desires that its presiding officer perform these and other similar functions, the bylaws should state these duties explicitly.

Only the elected president or, in his absence, a vice-president or the officer next in succession should preside at any meeting or convention where business may come before the assembly. If no officers are present at a meeting, a senior member calls the meeting to order and a temporary chairman is elected. The program chairman, the chairman of the convention, or some other member may preside at social or nonbusiness meetings, but if business arises which requires a vote, the regular presiding officer should take the chair. The elected presiding officer and vice-presidents cannot delegate to other members their duty or right to preside.

# Chapter 17. OTHER OFFICERS AND
## THEIR DUTIES

## THE VICE-PRESIDENT

### When a Vice-President Presides

The vice-president presides during the absence of the president and takes the place of the presiding officer whenever it is necessary for the latter to leave the chair. For instance, if the president decides to engage in debate, he calls upon the vice-president to preside. The vice-president takes the chair when a motion is proposed which affects the president only and remains in the chair until the motion is disposed of.

The vice-president has only a few responsibilities laid down by parliamentary law, but in actual practice he is usually assigned other duties by the bylaws.

### Succession to Office of President

The vice-president assumes the duties of the president in case of the absence or incapacity of the president. He becomes president upon the death, resignation, or permanent incapacity of the president. The second and subsequent vice-presidents, if there are any, then assume the offices of the vice-presidents next above them, and a new vice-president may then be elected. When acting in place of the president, the vice-president has all of the powers, duties, privileges, and responsibilities of the president.

Some organizations have two or more vice-presidents. These officers frequently direct departments of work or study, head important committees, serve on the governing board, or have other duties specifically assigned to them by the bylaws.

## SECRETARY

### Duties of the Secretary

The secretary should take accurate notes of whatever business comes before an assembly and from these notes prepare minutes, which are the official record of the proceedings of the organization. He aids the chairman by keeping a record of all motions, reading resolutions or papers when directed, and calling the roll when the vote is taken by roll call. He should understand parliamentary procedure and be ready to take the presiding officer's place if the vice-president is not present, at least until another chairman has been elected. When the secretary is a member, he does not forfeit any rights of membership by reason of his office and may vote on all measures if he desires.

The chief duties of a secretary may be summarized as follows:

1. To keep a careful and authentic record of the proceedings of the organization.
2. To take notes so that he may furnish the exact wording of a motion or motions pending before the organization.

3. To search the minutes for information which may be requested by officers or members.

4. To prepare a roll of members and call it when necessary.

5. To call the meeting to order in the absence of the presiding officers.

6. To preserve all records, reports, and documents of the organization except those specifically assigned to the custody of others.

7. To provide the chairman at the beginning of each meeting with a detailed order of business, including a list of unfinished business, of committees which are to report, and of announcements.

8. To provide the chairman of each committee with a list of the members of his committee and with all the papers and instructions intended for it.

9. To read all papers that may be called for by the assembly.

10. To authenticate all records by his signature.

11. To bring to each meeting a copy of the constitution, bylaws, and standing rules of the organization, together with a list of the members of all standing and special committees.

12. To carry on the official correspondence of the organization.

## Corresponding Secretary

In many organizations the secretarial duties are divided between a recording secretary and a corresponding secretary. The corresponding secretary writes all official correspondence for the organization, answers all official letters, and keeps the file of correspondence of the organization.

## Executive Secretary

Most national and state organizations and many local ones have an executive secretary. This officer is a paid official and may or may not be a member of the organization. He is chosen for his ability as an administrator and as an organizing expert. He is usually appointed by the governing board or committee and serves under their direction. He heads the business office of the organization, acts as an assistant to officers and committees, and serves as a valuable aid in maintaining a continuity of policy in organizations whose officers change annually or biennially.

## TREASURER

### Duties and Qualifications of the Treasurer

The treasurer is official custodian of the funds of the organization and also disbursing officer. As custodian, he is responsible for placing the organization's funds in a bank and for keeping an accurate record of the source of all moneys. As disbursing officer, he is responsible for the payment of all bills or of all warrants or requisitions, after payment is authorized. He is responsible for keeping a record of money paid out and of receipts or vouchers to cover each expenditure.

A treasurer should be chosen for his ability to keep books and for his financial integrity. He submits a summary of the finances of the organization at each meeting, if called for, and a complete report at least annually.

### Report of Treasurer

The report of the treasurer is always accompanied by such supporting records as accounts, warrants, checks, and vouchers. The annual report of the treasurer is ordinarily not accepted by the assembly but is referred to an auditing committee. The auditing committee is required to report at the annual meeting or the last meeting of the organization's year. It is a protection both to the organization and to the treasurer to have all financial records audited at least once annually.

The treasurer's annual report must be complete, but the summary or brief report read at each meeting is for the information of the members and should be simple. Details tend to confuse and are unnecessary, since their correctness is the concern of the auditing committee.

Except for the annual report, a brief summary of the following facts is usually sufficient:

### Receipts

Balance on hand at date of last report ..........
Receipts since last report ......................
Total .......................................

### Disbursements

Main items of expenditure ....................
Total disbursements ..........................
Present balance ..............................

The auditors or auditing committee submit a signed report certifying to the correctness of the treasurer's report. The auditors' report is voted upon and after its adoption, the treasurer is relieved of all financial responsibility for the time covered by his report, except where fraud exists.

## Financial Affairs of an Organization

The financial affairs of an organization should be conducted according to sound business practices. The treasurer is primarily responsible for the financial records of an organization.

Ordinarily funds are kept in a bank, and payments—except petty cash—are made by check. Checks are usually required to bear the signatures of the principal executive officer—the president or the executive secretary—and the treasurer.

Whenever there is a change in officers, a resolution should be passed authorizing the appropriate new officers to sign checks (unless that point is specifically covered in the by-laws) and an official notice should be sent to the bank.

No financial obligations should be incurred unless clearly authorized; and no payments should be made without prior authorization. Bills are usually submitted to a meeting (or to a board of directors where there is such a board and if it has been given that authority) for approval before payment is made.

Officers who handle money should be bonded. This is a protection to the officers as well as to the organization. A bonding company will explain the procedure necessary to secure a bond.

## PARLIAMENTARIAN

### Duties of the Parliamentarian

The parliamentarian serves as the president's adviser and consultant on procedural matters. Frequently a presiding officer must make decisions quickly and needs the advice of someone who is an authority on parliamentary procedure. The parliamentarian does not give his advice to the assembly but to the presiding officer.

The parliamentarian is a source of information on parliamentary procedure, but has no authority to enforce his ideas or rulings. Both the presiding officer and the organization may disregard the advice of the parliamentarian. Any inquiry on parliamentary procedure is addressed to the presiding officer and after consultation with the parliamentarian, if he wishes, the presiding officer answers the inquiry.

The parliamentarian unobtrusively calls the attention of the presiding officer to any serious error in procedure which he observes. As far as possible, he should anticipate difficult situations and keep the presiding officer advised concerning questions in dispute or points of order. In conventions and in large organizations the parliamentarian is a paid technical adviser acting in a capacity similar to that of an attorney.

## SERGEANT AT ARMS

The sergeant at arms, under the direction of the presiding officer, maintains order and decorum among the members and all persons present at a meeting and may even expel persons from the meeting. He may act as doorkeeper and is responsible for admitting only eligible persons. He acts as usher or directs the ushers and is generally responsible for the comfort and convenience of the assembly. In some organizations it is his duty to arrange the meeting equipment, such as chairs and tables. In small organizations he may perform these duties personally, but in large organizations he may have a staff of assistant sergeants at arms. In some organizations the sergeant at arms is a paid, permanent official.

## HONORARY OFFICERS

Some organizations provide in their bylaws for honorary officers and honorary members. These honorary titles are created as a compliment to those upon whom they are conferred, and generally carry with them the right to attend meetings and to speak but not to propose motions, to vote, or to preside. The holding of an honorary office does not preclude a person who is also a regular member from holding a regular office. Honorary status is perpetual unless rescinded; consequently, the names of deceased honorary officers and members are often included in the published roster of an organization.

## Chapter 18. COMMITTEES

### Value of Committees

The bulk of the actual work of most organizations is done by committees. The meetings of many organizations are concerned largely with the consideration of committee reports. Ideas are formulated by committees for final decision by the whole assembly, and work is delegated to committees to be carried out and reported back to the assembly. The work of an organization is thus apportioned among groups of members who are responsible to all the members for its accomplishment. Usually the decisions and conclusions of committees are accepted as the decisions and conclusions of the organization. Thus committees are the most important working force of organizations.

Committee work is the training school in which members prepare for executive duties in the larger organization. Committees provide the best opportunity for testing and proving ability to work and to lead.

### Advantages of Committees

A committee has many advantages which enable it to work more efficiently than the larger parent organization. Among these advantages are:

1. Greater freedom of discussion is possible.
2. A longer time may be devoted to each subject.
3. Informal procedure is possible because of the small number present.
4. Better use can be made of the knowledge of experts.
5. Delicate and troublesome questions may be studied or investigated without publicity.
6. In committee hearings nonmembers, as well as members, can be permitted to express their views.

## Special Committees and Standing Committees

There are two main classes of committees, special committees and standing committees.

A special committee is selected to perform some specific task and ceases to exist when its final report is submitted. The assembly may, however, vote to delegate additional work to the committee, in which case it continues until the new assignment is completed and a further report is submitted. A committee to have charge of the annual banquet is an example of a special committee.

A standing committee is chosen to perform any work in a particular field that may be referred to it over a fixed period of time. Usually this period of time coincides with the terms of the officers of the organization. Standing committees furnish an ever ready and experienced group to which subjects within their scope may be referred at any time. They also enable an organization to delegate many tasks which need to be carried out regularly. A membership committee, which investigates and passes upon all applications for membership in the organization, is an example of a standing committee.

## Committees for Deliberation and Committees for Action

Committees may also be classified, according to their

work, into committees for deliberation and committees for action. It is vital that committees appointed for deliberation and investigation represent every important element and group of the organization. Thus the report of the committee will reflect the opinion of the whole organization. A committee to determine the need for a new bridge is an example of an investigating and deliberative committee.

Committees for action, on the contrary, are appointed to carry out a particular task already determined upon and function best when composed entirely of persons who favor the work to be undertaken. A committee to raise a sick benefit fund is an example of a committee for action.

## Selection of Committees

Committees may be elected by the organization or appointed by the presiding officer or by the governing board. The manner of their selection is determined either by the bylaws or by the motion creating the committee.

A president usually asks the advice of other members when appointing committees. Members of executive boards, boards of directors, and advisory committees usually have a wide knowledge of members and their abilities and can advise the president advantageously. Consultation with them will enable the president to enlist the support and utilize the talents of a large number of members.

It is advisable to consult a committee chairman regarding the selection of the other members of his committee. Particularly when a committee is assigned a difficult problem or task, the chairman is entitled to have a voice in the selection of the committee members.

## Selection of Committee Chairmen

A committee chairman should be chosen carefully for his ability to handle the particular work of his committee. The chairman of a committee is a very important officer because, unlike the chairman of an assembly, he takes an active part in all discussions and deliberations. When the committee chairman is not elected by the organization or appointed by the chairman, he may be selected by the committee itself from its own membership. There is no parliamentary rule which requires that the member who proposes the creation of a committee be appointed the chairman.

If no chairman of a committee is designated, the member first named should call the committee together and preside until the election of a chairman.

## Ex-officio Members of Committees

In some organizations the bylaws provide that the president or some other officer shall be a member of one or more committees because of the particular office which he holds. The officer is then called an ex-officio member of the committees.

Ex-officio members of committees are provided for in order to make available to the committee the particular information in the possession of the ex-officio member, or to coordinate the work of the committee with the work of his office. The establishment of an ex-officio membership may also be for the purpose of giving to the officer—usually the president—a tighter control over a certain committee or a group of committees. A provision making the head of an organization an ex-officio member of all committees is sometimes made, but is rarely, if ever, advantageous.

A treasurer of an organization, for example, could be very helpful to a finance committee, and his participation in the work of the committee should make its work more effective and its decisions more reliable.

An ex-officio member of a committee has all the rights and responsibilities of any other committee member. When an ex-officio member ceases to hold office, his membership on a committee terminates automatically.

## Instructions to Committees

Committees should be given specific information and instructions concerning the work which they are expected to do. A copy of any motion or resolution referred to the committee is given to the chairman or secretary of the committee. To proceed efficiently, important committees should receive from the secretary all information in his possession which would be of assistance to the committee.

Such information may include the following items:

1. List of committee members
2. Motion, resolution, or paper referred to the committee
3. Any specific instructions to the committee from the assembly
4. All available papers relating to the subject assigned the committee
5. Definition of the scope of authority of the committee
6. Statement of any policies, rules, or decisions of the assembly relating to the subject
7. Date when the committee report is due

## Powers, Rights, and Duties of Committees

The powers, rights, and duties of committees should be specifically provided for in the constitution, bylaws, or standing rules of an organization or in the motions which create the committees. Even an executive committee has no power except that delegated to it by vote or by the constitution or bylaws. No committee has inherent rights or duties. All rights and all duties must be delegated to it by the parent organization.

## Work of Committees

A committee's work may consist of the consideration of a motion or a problem referred to it or an investigation of a subject or the accomplishment of work delegated to it by the organization or a combination of any of these.

It is the duty of a committee chairman to familiarize his members with the policies of the organization and to make sure that they work in harmony with those policies. A committee cannot change a policy of the organization and should be careful to conform to any policies already fixed. A committee never makes representations of any kind to any outside person or organization except when specifically authorized or when these representations are clearly within the policy of the organization.

The work of committees can be made more effective by providing each committee member, in advance of the meeting, with an agenda showing all questions to be considered at the meeting. Information which is to be considered by the committee, such as reports or studies to be passed upon at the meeting, should also be supplied to committee members so that they may become familiar with the problems to be solved and with the material bearing upon the solution, and so that they may have an opportunity to give thought beforehand to the questions to be decided.

No committee should be appointed unless it has work to do, for members included on a committee which has no real work are soon discouraged. The task should already exist before a committee is created to carry it out.

## Procedure in Committee Meetings

Since one of the objects of creating committees is to permit informal discussion, simple committee procedure is desirable.

Committees follow the ordinary rules of procedure insofar as they are appropriate to the particular committee situation, but most of their proceedings should be very informal. There is one motion which must always be proposed and voted upon in regular parliamentary form. This is the motion adopting or approving the report or recommendations to be made by the committee.

In small committee meetings it is not necessary to stand when making a motion or to require seconds or to wait for recognition by the chairman before speaking or to limit the length of speeches or for the chairman to leave the chair when discussing a motion.

To expedite the work of a committee, motions or questions must be accurately stated before discussion begins. Discussion is confined to the motion or question, and only one person is permitted to speak at a time. In large committees when considering important and highly controversial subjects, it may be necessary at times to be almost as formal and to apply parliamentary rules substantially as strictly as in the assembly itself.

Unless otherwise specified, a majority of the members of a committee constitutes a quorum, and a majority of the legal votes cast is necessary to take any official action.

Meetings of a committee should be called by the chairman, and in case of his inability or failure to act, by any two members of the committee.

If no secretary is provided, minutes should be kept by one member who is delegated to act as secretary. These minutes are for the benefit and convenience of the committee only and are not open to the inspection of anyone who is not a committee member.

Minutes of committee meetings may be more detailed than those of the parent organization. Minutes of hearings should list the name of all persons who appear before the committee, and it is often advantageous to summarize all arguments presented. This record is frequently useful in preparing the committee's recommendations.

A committee may appoint subcommittees of its own members which are directly responsible to the committee and which have no power except that delegated to them by the committee. Such subcommittees report only to the committee which created them.

## Amendments by Committee

When a motion or resolution is referred to a committee while there are amendments pending, the amendments are considered by the committee and recommendations made concerning them.

When a committee proposes amendments to any motion or to any resolution, or other paper which has been referred to it, the amendments are not inserted in the proposition but are proposed separately. A committee cannot amend a proposition referred to it but can only propose amendments. Amendments can be adopted only by the assembly.

When a motion or resolution referred to a committee requires extensive amendment, the committee may rewrite the proposal and recommend that it be substituted for the original.

## Committee Hearings

If the question to be considered by a committee involves a general question of policy, the committee may hold hearings which are usually open to all members of the organization. A reasonable opportunity should be given to all members to express their views before the committee. Ample notice of committee hearings is desirable to enable any member to attend the discussion of any question in which he is interested, unless the committee has been given instructions for private hearings. During regular deliberations of a committee, no one except members of the committee has the right to be present unless invited by the committee.

## Content and Form of Committee Reports

Committee reports may consist of the following:

1. A statement of the question referred to the committee or of the subject reported upon or of the purpose of the committee study or investigation
2. The scope of the action or work of the committee or the manner in which the study or investigation was conducted
3. The information or testimony received by the committee or a summary of information or testimony
4. Findings or conclusions
5. Recommendations

Resolutions to carry out the recommendations may be submitted with the report, but should not be a part of it. The committee should prepare and submit separately all resolutions necessary to carry out its recommendations.

When a committee has been appointed to carry out an assignment of work, the report states concisely what was done and gives such information as will be desirable to have in the records.

A committee report gives credit to anyone rendering special or outstanding service to the committee, but does not give special mention to anyone who only performs his duties well.

A committee report should be as brief as is consistent with clarity. It should give the background necessary to an understanding of the recommendations. When the committee has made a study or conducted an investigation, a summary of the information upon which the conclusions or recommendations are based is included. When the report is long, the principal points are summarized before the conclusions.

## Agreeing upon Committee Reports

The report of a committe must be agreed upon at a meeting of the committee. This is because the report is to express the collective judgment of the committee, and it is essential that the members have the opportunity to discuss freely with each other the questions involved in the report. The approval of a committee report by members individually and separately, without a meeting, is not a valid approval. There are no exceptions to this rule unless they are stated in the bylaws.

When it is very difficult or impossible for the members of a committee to meet, the bylaws—or a resolution or motion—may make provision for the committee to agree on a report without a meeting. The report may be prepared embodying the opinion of the members of the committee as far as it can be determined, and submitted by mail or otherwise to the members for their approval. Members approving sign the report to indicate their approval; or they may approve with reservations or exceptions. When thus provided for, a report approved by a majority of the committee members may be presented as the report of the committee. It is important that every member of the committee who can possibly be reached have the opportunity to review the proposed report and to present to the other members of the committee or to the organization any objections they may have. A member may withdraw his approval of a report at any time before it is presented.

When the report in its final form has been considered by the committee and officially approved by a majority vote, it is authenticated by the signature of the chairman. If the report has not been considered and voted upon in final form at a committee meeting, it must be signed by at least a majority of the members of the committee, and it is desirable that it be signed by all members who agree to it.

## Presentation of Committee Reports

The order of business makes provision for the presentation of committee reports. When the time for the consideration of committee reports arrives, the presiding officer calls for reports of committees. Standing committees usually report first in the order in which they are listed in the rules or bylaws and are followed by special committees in the order of their appointment.

A committee report is presented by its chairman or some other member of the committee selected by the committee or designated by the committee chairman for that purpose. He may make such remarks or present such information as seems to him necessary to explain the report or to introduce it properly. The report is then read by the person presenting it or by the secretary. After the reading of the report, the person presenting it may move, if he chooses, that it be filed or that it be adopted.

When a long committee report is presented, the entire report may not be read, but in order to conserve the time of the assembly, only the summary, conclusions, and recommendations. If reports are properly prepared, this is a satisfactory procedure.

In organizations having annual conventions, committees are frequently required to present their reports in advance, and they are printed and distributed to members at the convention. It is not necessary or desirable to read the printed report at the convention. The person presenting the report makes only such introductory or explanatory statements as may be required and refers to the printed report.

A committee report may be called for and presented prior

to the time fixed for its presentation by a motion to suspend the rules, which requires a two-thirds vote. When a report is called for, its presentation may be postponed to a later time by a motion to postpone definitely. Until the time arrives for which the committee report is scheduled, no postponement of the time of reporting is permissible except by a motion to suspend the rules. By unanimous consent committee reports are usually presented in the order which is most convenient for the assembly or for committee chairmen.

## Consideration of Committee Reports

A committee report, after being presented to an assembly, is subject to debate as though it were a motion or resolution. The report may be severely criticized, but the members of the committee or their motives may not be attacked. If extensive discussion of a report develops, the presiding officer may facilitate the discussion by requiring that the report be considered paragraph by paragraph or recommendation by recommendation.

A committee report cannot be amended. The report can be accepted as a whole or in part, or with exceptions or reservations. The best procedure is to present any recommendations separately as resolutions or motions, and to submit the report only for the information of the members.

The resolutions submitted by a committee with its report are acted upon individually and are subject to the same rules as other main motions.

## Disposition of Committee Reports

If recommendations are included in the report they should be stated at the end of the report. When so stated, they can be considered either as a group or individually and can be either accepted or rejected, or accepted with exceptions or limitations; or entirely different decisions can be made on the subjects dealt with in the report.

The report of a committee, or the recommendations made as a part of the report, cannot be amended because they are the words of the committee and the organization cannot make the committee say something it did not say. The organization need not accept the recommendations and can make its own decisions on all questions covered by the committee report or recommendations. Motions and resolutions are proposals for actions or statements by the organization itself and so can be amended to make them express the will of the organization.

A committee report, after presentation, may be disposed of in any of the following ways:

1. The report may be filed. It may be ordered filed by a motion, or if no motion is presented, the presiding officer may announce, "The report will be filed," and proceed to the next item of business. Reports containing information only and reports of progress are filed and are not adopted. A report which is filed is not binding on the assembly but is available for the information of the members.

2. A subject and the report covering it may be referred back to the committee if it is not satisfactory to the assembly or if it is believed further study, modification, or recommendations should be made.

3. Consideration of a committee report, after it has been presented, may be postponed to a more convenient time.

4. A report may be adopted. When a report is adopted, the assembly is committed to all the findings contained in the report and to any recommendations included in it but not to any recommendations submitted separately.

5. A report may be rejected. The question on a report should always be put in positive form ("I move the report be adopted"), but a negative vote on a motion to adopt would have the effect of rejecting the report.

6. A committee report can be adopted in part or with exceptions or reservations.

7. A final or annual financial report from a treasurer, board, or committee is referred to the auditors or auditing committee by the presiding officer without a motion. No such report is adopted. Adoption of the report of the auditors or auditing committee certifying to the correctness of the report is equivalent to approval of a financial report.

If the organization has no provision for auditors or an auditing committee, a motion to elect an auditing committee or to authorize the chairman to appoint one is in order.

If the financial report concerns proposed or future expenditures only, it is treated as any other report containing recommendations.

## Danger in Adopting Committee Reports

Since the adoption of a committee report binds the assembly to recommendations contained in the report, organizations frequently find themselves committed on matters that have received little consideration by the assembly. Recommendations should be submitted separately from the report, but they are sometimes included in it. Therefore, it is essential that, in adopting any report, all recommendations and conclusions in it be carefully read and considered by the assembly before the report is adopted. Instead of adopting committee reports, a better and safer policy is to receive and file them for the information of the organization and to require in the bylaws that all recommendations be presented in separate resolutions for decision by vote of the assembly.

The word "accept" is sometimes used instead of "adopt" to indicate the approval or adoption of a committee report. In the interest of clarity, however, the word "adopt," which is never misunderstood, should be used instead of "accept," which is sometimes confused with "receive." To "receive" a report does not commit or bind the assembly to any findings or recommendations contained in the report.

## Duration of Committees

The following rules govern the existence and termination of special committees:

1. When a final report is submitted, a special committee automatically ceases to exist.
2. When a partial report is submitted, the committee continues.
3. When a final report is submitted and the matter is again referred to the committee, the committee is revived.
4. When the organization decides by a majority vote to withdraw a subject from a special committee, the committee is automatically terminated.

A standing committee is appointed at the beginning of a new administration and continues until the next election of officers. A subject may be withdrawn from a standing committee by majority vote of the organization, but this action does not affect the life of the committee.

## Record of Committee Reports

When a report of a committee or officer is read, it is handed to the secretary. It is the duty of the secretary or recording secretary to file all reports after each meeting in such a manner that they are available to officers and members. The approved method is to file them in a special book or file reserved for that purpose.

Reports of each standing committee should be filed in chronological order under the title of the committee, whereas reports of special committees should be filed in alphabetical order according to subject matter and indexed under the name of the committee.

The minutes of each meeting state what reports were presented, by whom, and the disposition of each report. The minutes also record the page number in the report book or the heading in the file where the particular report may be found.

## Minority Reports

If any members of a committee disagree with the report submitted by the majority of the committee members, they may submit a minority report signed by those members who agree to it. More than one minority report may be submitted. If there is a minority report, it should be presented immediately after the majority report. A minority has the right to present a report, even though a motion is pending to dispose of the majority report. Objection can be made to receiving a minority report in the same way that a main motion may be objected to.

The minority report is presented by one of its sponsors in the same manner as a majority report, but is not considered unless a member moves to substitute it for the report of the majority. If this motion receives a majority vote, the minority report becomes the report of the committee, and the majority report is filed for reference. If the motion to substitute fails to carry, the minority report is defeated, although it should be filed for reference.

A member who agrees with a committee report with exceptions or reservations may indicate those matters with which he does not agree and sign the report, signifying his approval of the remainder of the report.

## Committee of the Whole

When a legislative body wishes to proceed informally, it resolves itself into a committee of the whole and becomes subject to the less formal procedure of a committee. An advantage of this procedure is that persons not members of the organization may be permitted to appear and speak. A disadvantage is that the regular presiding officer must relinquish the chair and call upon some other person to preside. Also, it is necessary to vote upon a committee report. The same purpose is served much more simply in ordinary organizations by the more modern use of informal consideration, as explained on page 49.

## Executive Committee or Board

An executive committee, board of managers, board of trustees, or governing board is a small deliberative assembly and derives all of its powers from the parent organization. It has only such authority as is given to it by the constitution or bylaws or is voted to it from time to time by the organization. It does not have any inherent powers. Its time of meetings, quorum, duties, powers, officers, and procedure are usually determined and defined by the organization from which the committee derives.

Such a committee or board is usually given the authority to act, within limitations, for the whole organization during the periods when the organization is not in session.

Because of the important powers frequently given an executive board, members are usually elected or the board i composed, at least in part, of elected officers of the organi zation. A board is organized with a chairman and a secretary who are sometimes elected by the board but are frequentl chairman and secretary of the parent body. Some organizations elect a certain number of the members of the executive committee each year, staggering their terms of office so that there are always some members who have had previous experience on the board. Other organizations prefer to elect an entirely new board with each incoming president on the theory that the new presiding officer can work best with a new board.

An executive committee or board should make a complete report of its activities at least annually.

# Chapter 19. RIGHTS OF MEMBERS

## Fundamental Rights of Members

It is important that each member understand his individual and his joint rights so that he may protect them.

Certain rights are fundamental and inherent in the right of membership, but an organization may, in its rules, give whatever additional rights it chooses to its members.

Each member of an organization has the following fundamental rights, subject only to specific limitations or restrictions contained in the constitution, bylaws, or standing rules:

1. To receive notices
2. To attend meetings
3. To speak
4. To vote
5. To present motions, resolutions, or other business
6. To nominate
7. To be a candidate or run for office
8. To resign, if all obligations to the organization have been fulfilled
9. To have a hearing before expulsion or other penalties are applied

10. To inspect official records of the organization
11. To insist on the enforcement of the rules of the organization and the rules of parliamentary law
12. To exercise any other rights given by the constitution or rules of the organization

## Membership in Organizations

The general rule is that every voluntary organization has complete authority to grant or refuse membership in the organization,[1] to make rules governing the admission of members,[2] and to place restrictions on membership.[3] For example, the name of a prospective member may be required to be submitted at the meeting in advance of voting on his admission to membership, or the total membership may be limited to fifty.

An exception to the rule that any voluntary association can refuse membership to anyone it wishes is that certain trade associations and unions cannot refuse membership to persons who would suffer economic loss thereby.

In the absence of a rule to the contrary, a member may resign or withdraw at his pleasure, and no acceptance of his resignation is necessary.[4] When the bylaws or rules provide a procedure for terminating membership, that procedure must be followed.[5] For example, it is sometimes provided that no member can resign until all dues have been paid up to date.

## Legal Relations of Organizations and Members

When a member joins an organization, he establishes a relationship between himself and the organization on the basis of a contract. No particular procedure is necessary so long as a mutual understanding as to membership is reached.[6] Some organizations may require members to sign the constitution and bylaws. In other organizations an applicant becomes a member the moment his application is approved.

When a person joins an organization, he accepts the organization as it then is, and the organization accepts him, and he becomes subject to the constitution, bylaws, and rules of the organization as they then exist.[7]

Under the principles of the common law, the member and the organization are both bound by the rules of parliamentary law.[8] They are bound by the constitution and bylaws or charter and any rules of the organization which were in effect when the member joined. All of these are a part of the contract binding both.

## Change in Rights of Members

The rights of members do not necessarily remain unchanged. Certain privileges which all members had might be taken away, or fees and dues might be increased. The constitution or bylaws may be changed in any authorized manner so long as the fundamental purposes of the organization are not changed or vested rights destroyed.[9] Changes in the constitution or bylaws must be made according to rules contained in the constitution or bylaws.[10]

## Expulsion of Members

Every organization has inherent power to suspend or expel a member for cause.[11] An organization also has authority to make rules for the suspension or expulsion of members.[12] The power to expel is often set forth in the bylaws, and when it is so set forth, is binding on both the members and the organization.[13]

In general, a membership can be terminated because of the member's violation of a duty to the organization or a breach of the organization's rules.[14]

An organization has the implied power to expel a member

for violation of his duty as a member or as a citizen. The following are examples of such instances:

1. Conviction of an offense so infamous as to render the member unfit for the society of "honest men." [15]
2. When a member has committed some offense in violation of his duty as a member.[16]
3. When the member's conduct violates the fundamental objects of the association and when such conduct, if continued, would bring the organization into disrepute.[17]
4. When the member has violated some rule which is set forth in the bylaws or rules as a ground for expulsion.[18]

A proceeding to expel a member must not violate any rules of the organization nor violate the member's rights under the common law.[19] The primary requisities for expulsion are due notice and hearing. The notice must be adequate to acquaint the member with the charges so that he may prepare his defense.[20]

A member is entitled to a hearing before a fair and impartial group, who are acting in good faith, and to an opportunity to present his evidence and to refute evidence presented against him.[21] It is not necessary that the technical legal rules of evidence be followed as in a trial in court.[22]

# Chapter 20. MEETINGS

## Meetings, Conventions, and Conferences

A meeting is an assemblage of the members of an organization for any length of time, during which there is no separation of the members except for a recess. It consists of the period between the time a group convenes and the time it adjourns. A meeting which has been recessed is resumed at the point at which it was interrupted; but when a meeting has been adjourned it is terminated, and the next meeting is opened with the usual formalities of a new meeting.

A group of meetings, spoken of collectively or as a unit, is often called a "convention" or a "conference." The terms "convention" or "conference" refer to the gathering of a group of people for a series of meetings which follow in close succession.

The term "session" has two distinct meanings. It may refer to a single meeting, as "a morning session" or "an evening session," or it may refer to a series of meetings, as to a "session of Congress." Because of this confusion, the term "session" is not used in this book.

Most organizations have a monthly or weekly meeting and an annual conference or convention.

## Regular Meetings

Organizations usually have a fixed time and place for holding meetings, which are ordinarily named in the bylaws or standing rules. Such meetings held in compliance with these regulations are regular meetings. Since members are presumed to be familiar with the bylaws and rules, no additional notice of these meetings need be given unless the bylaws or rules specifically provide for further notice. Rules governing the giving of notice of meetings have been strictly construed by the courts and unless the required notice is given the meeting can take no valid action.

No change in the regular time or place of meetings established by rule or custom can be legally made without notice to all the members.

At any regular meeting any business which comes within the scope of the organization can be transacted.

It is important when adjourning a meeting that there is no confusion as to whether the next meeting is to be a special meeting, an adjourned meeting, or a regular meeting.

When a meeting is adjourned to the time of the next regular meeting, that meeting is the regular meeting and not an adjourned meeting.

## Special Meetings

A special meeting is a meeting not regularly scheduled which is held to transact definite and specified business. The bylaws usually provide a method for calling special meetings. A special meeting can be called only as authorized in the bylaws. Usually the presiding officer or the executive board may call a special meeting and must call such a meeting upon the written request of a certain number of members.

A special meeting is always subject to certain restrictions:

1. Every member of the organization must be notified of the meeting. If it is established that any member was omitted from the list of members notified, the transactions of the meeting are not valid.[1] A meeting at which all members are present and participate is legal despite defects in the notice.

2. The call or notice for a special meeting must state all items of business which the meeting is to consider. Stating the business which is to be considered in general language such as "any other proper business" is not legal.[2] The list as stated in the call forms the order of business for the special meeting. A copy of the call should be inserted in the minutes.

3. When the special meeting convenes, it cannot consider any business not specified in the call for the meeting.

## Adjourned Meetings

When it is desirable to continue a regular or special meeting at a later time, a motion to adjourn or to recess the meeting to that time makes the second meeting an adjourned meeting of the first. Adjourned meetings may themselves be adjourned to later adjourned meetings. No adjourned meeting may be set for a time which is later than the time of convening the next regular meeting.

There are two occasions when an adjourned meeting may be necessary or desirable. These are:

1. When there is not time to transact all business at a regular or special meeting, it is more convenient to complete the unfinished business at an adjourned meeting rather than at another special meeting. This procedure eliminates the necessity of the special notice which would be required for the second meeting.

2. When it is desirable that a meeting be in session after

a particular event or happening, the regular or special meeting can be adjourned until after that time and then reconvene as an adjourned meeting. For example, if an organization has called a special meeting to decide whether to build a new clubhouse and it is found that more information is needed on costs, the meeting might be adjourned until the information is secured.

An adjourned meeting is legally a continuation of the previous regular or special meeting. The interval between the adjournment and the reconvening of the adjourned meeting is, in effect, a recess. Any business which was pending at the time the original meeting adjourned is still pending when the adjourned meeting is called to order.[3]

The organization can do any business at the adjourned meeting which might have been done if no adjournment had been taken. Limitations on the organization at the original meeting remain in force at the adjourned meeting and an adjourned special meeting can transact only such business as could have been transacted at the special meeting.

# Chapter 21. CONVENTIONS

*Preparation for Conventions*

The success of a convention is greatly influenced by the efficiency of its preliminary planning. The task of planning and "putting on" a convention is carried out by administrative committees which are usually appointed at the previous convention, or shortly thereafter, and are chosen by the executive board or by the president.

The following committees are frequently appointed:

| | | | |
|---|---|---|---|
| 1. | Credentials | 7. | Decorations |
| 2. | Registration | 8. | Courtesy |
| 3. | Program | 9. | Arrangements |
| 4. | Resolutions | 10. | Housing |
| 5. | Entertainment | 11. | Rules |
| 6. | Transportation | 12. | Public Relations |

Committees on decoration, arrangement, entertainment, housing, and courtesy are usually supplemented by local committees or members. The work, or plans for the work, of all of these committees should be completed prior to the convention.

## Accrediting of Delegates

The most important business of an organization is decided by its delegates at its conventions. It is, therefore, important that all delegates be carefully accredited.

There are many methods of accrediting delegates. The following is one efficient method:

The number of delegates to which each unit or district is entitled is determined. The head office sends two copies of delegates' cards for each allotted delegate to the president or secretary of the local unit. The card states that the person whose signature appears on the card is the duly elected representative of that unit. This credential card is signed by the local president or secretary, or both. One of the cards is given to the delegate and the other is returned to the head office, together with the necessary registration fees. Alternates' credentials are handled in the same manner.

At the assigned time each delegate reports to the headquarters of the credentials committee and presents his credential card, fills out a registration card, and receives his badge and other convention material.

Lost credentials are replaced by identification and certification of the delegate to the credentials office by some officer of the local unit.

No person is admitted to any meeting of a convention without presenting his credentials.

## Seating of Delegates

Time will be conserved and confusion avoided if carefully drawn, detailed rules for the seating of delegates, alternates, observers, visitors, and others are rigidly observed. In recognizing speakers and in taking votes, it is important that the presiding officer and others know exactly which

persons are the accredited delegates. A section of the hall
is reserved for delegates and must be restricted to delegates
only. Alternates are not seated with the delegates unless a
delegate is absent, in which case his alternate is seated in the
delegate's place. Members in good standing who are not
delegates may sit in a separate place and observers and
visitors in another.

Ushers should require all persons to show their credentials
before taking their seats. Walking about the convention floor
and entering sections to which a member is not accredited
must be prevented. Pages should be available to do necessary
errands.

The privileges of nonvoting members should be specifically
defined.

## Report of Credentials Committee

After the opening ceremonies, which usually consist of
an invocation and speeches of welcome and responses, the
first official business is the consideration of the report of the
credentials committee so that it may be known who is entitled to vote. The credentials committee ordinarily is able
to give only a preliminary report at the opening meeting.
This committee's report is usually made up of a list of the
delegates and their alternates and the ex-officio members of
the convention who are present. Ex-officio members usually
consist of the officers of the convention, the chairmen of the
committees which planned the convention, and the members
of the executive board.

The report of the credentials committee, like all other
reports, is read by the committee chairman or by the convention secretary. When the motion to adopt the report has
carried, the list of accredited delegates contained in the report becomes the official roll of those entitled to vote.

Supplementary reports by the credentials and program committees may be necessary, and these are given at the beginning of any meeting.

## Report of Rules Committee

Following the report of the credentials committee, which establishes who is to vote, the committee on rules of the convention submits its report so that delegates may have a clear understanding of the working rules of the convention. Since the rules ordinarily vary only slightly from year to year, the report of the rules committee is frequently published beforehand, often as a part of the program, and distributed to each delegate.

The rules are adopted by a majority vote and can be suspended at any time by a two-thirds vote. Rules of conventions differ widely but frequently cover such subjects as the following: registration of delegates, guest speakers, attendance of guests and observers, seating of delegates, alternates, and guests, use of proxies, length of speeches, past officers, how motions and resolutions may be introduced, how resolutions are assigned to committees, the privileges of nonvoting members and visitors, and any special rules peculiar to the convention.

## Order of Business or Program

The program committee, working with the executive board, usually prepares and prints the convention program. This is submitted for approval at the first meeting of the body and, once adopted, becomes the official order of business for the convention. When an order of business has been adopted, it is the duty of the presiding officer to see that it is followed. It can be deviated from only by a majority vote or by unanimous consent unless the bylaws or rules provide otherwise.

## Standing Reference Committees

Many large conventions find that their business proceedings are handled most satisfactorily by means of standing reference committees. Instead of allowing any member to bring up any motion at any time, these organizations establish standing committees through which all new business must be introduced and filtered.

If a member wishes to propose a motion or resolution, he submits it in writing to the secretary or to the chairman of the appropriate committee. The committee considers it, and if the proposal receives a favorable majority vote of the committee, it is brought before the convention for its consideration. This procedure saves time, and the time of a convention is very valuable. When the reference committees are chosen wisely and are representative of all opinions and groups, the procedure of referring all matters to them is of great value to the convention in time saved, issues clarified, policies coordinated, and increased volume of business which it is possible to handle.

It is advantageous for a reference committee to be a standing committee of the organization rather than a convention committee in order that it may function prior to the convention. By providing beforehand for submission of proposals much confusion can be avoided and time saved at the convention.

## General Screening Committee

Another method of sifting and apportioning resolutions and motions is by the establishment of a single committee of reference, whose duty it is to screen all proposals for the consideration of the convention. Usually some of the members of such a committee are former officers. This committee receives all resolutions, motions, and petitions and determines whether they are suitable for consideration by the convention. Those proposals which meet the requirements are sent to the proper standing committee, whose duty it is to consider the subject covered by the motion, resolution, or petition.

The screening committee frequently clarifies motions and resolutions and corrects errors in them before referring them to the proper committee. The screening committee may refuse to accept proposals which, in its judgment, are unsuitable for the consideration of any committee or of the convention. In organizations which function under this type of screening committee, an appeal from the decision of the committee to the convention is usually permitted.

Some organizations have a complete and detailed order of business which has been planned in advance. When a motion, resolution, or communication which is not part of this detailed order of business is presented on the floor of the convention, it is automatically referred to a committee created for the purpose of deciding which questions are suitable for presentation to, and consideration by, the convention. An appeal from the decisions of this committee may be taken and a hearing may be held upon presentation to the secretary of a petition signed by a specified number of delegates.

## Minutes Committee

Most large organizations conserve time at their conventions by selecting a minutes or journal committee, whose duty it is to examine the record of the secretary, comparing it with the stenographic transcript, if there is one, and to report its finding and recommendations to the governing board. (For functions of the minutes committee see Chapter 15.)

## Committee on Public Relations

A committee on public relations is one of the most important committees of the convention. It has charge of newspaper, radio, and television publicity. When possible, this committee should include at least one member who is technically trained in public relations and the issuance of public information. If the convention has no members who are experienced in publicity work, it is desirable to secure a public relations representative to ensure that actions and opinions of the convention reach the public in effective form and that misunderstandings and misinterpretations are avoided.

A public relations committee sees that all newspapers, magazines, and news syndicates receive equal treatment in the distribution of news and equal opportunity to secure news. News releases are prepared in advance on important reports and speeches.

Space on the convention floor is set aside for the use of the press, and a room equipped with typewriters, copies of news releases, and telephones will help to maintain good press relations.

All press releases are issued by the public relations committee only, and all press relations are handled by this committee. This includes photographs, interviews, radio and television appearances, seats for banquets or social occasions, tickets of admission for the press, and letters of thanks.

If it is necessary to hold any meetings which are not open to the press, the representatives of the press should be notified previous to the meeting time that the meeting is to be a closed one.

## Official Minutes of Conventions

There are three forms of recording proceedings which conventions usually use:

1. A verbatim report by a professional reporter
2. Minutes prepared and approved by the secretary, minutes committee, or other authorized persons
3. Abstract of the minutes prepared for publication

The official record of the convention consists of the minutes prepared by the secretary and approved according to the requirements of the organization.

The record of the reporter is a record of everything that is said. The minutes of the secretary is a complete record of every action taken. The abstract of the minutes is a short résumé of important actions taken and is intended for publication as a report to those members who did not attend the convention.

## Roll Call of Delegates

Conventions save considerable time and avoid an initial roll call by checking delegates as they enter the convention hall. If delegates are restricted to one or two doors for entrance, a registration desk may be placed at each door. Each desk is in charge of a member of the credentials committee, who has a list of all delegates. As each delegate enters the hall, he presents his credentials, and his name is checked on the list. If he leaves the hall before the termination of the meeting, his name is checked off the list. By combining the lists from the different entrances, it is possible to tell at any given moment which delegates and how many are in attendance. If a roll call is ordered on a vote, this list serves as the list for the roll call.

## Recognizing Members

In conventions it is difficult for the presiding officer to know the names and districts of all delegates. To save time and to keep the record clear, each delegate or alternate, as soon as he is recognized, gives his name and the organization or district which he represents, as for example, "Mr. A from San Francisco" or "Mr. M from Florida."

Since the minutes of conventions usually include the names of the seconder of a motion or resolution, a delegate who rises to second a motion also gives his name and the name of the group which he represents. In controversial discussions, when it is desirable that both sides or opinions be represented as equitably as possible, each speaker, in requesting recognition, may be asked by the presiding officer to state whether he is for or against the motion before the assembly so that the presiding officer may alternate speeches between sides of a controversy.

## Committee Reports

Committee reports are prepared and presented to conventions in the same manner as to other meetings of an organization. (For rules governing committee reports, see Chapter 18.)

## Voting in Conventions

In large organizations voting is sometimes done by delegations. The chairman of the delegation knows his delegates and is able to take a vote quickly. The chairman of each delegation polls his delegation and reports the results when the roll of delegations is called. Thus the process of voting is speeded up and confusion in voting is minimized. Conventions follow all the rules governing voting as explained in Chapter 10.

## Special Guests and Guest Speakers

Uniform rules for the seating of speakers, honored guests, and past officers, both at banquets and on the platform, prevent misunderstandings and injured feelings. The committee that has charge of guests and guest speakers attends to all details which will make the guest speaker more comfortable. These include notifying him what type of dress will be worn, whether he may bring anyone with him, at what hour he is expected to arrive, how his transportation will be arranged, how long he is expected to speak, other speakers who are to appear on the program and their subjects, at what place on the program he is to speak, where he is to stay if a guest of the convention, and any facts about the organization or its history, policies, or beliefs which would be of help to him in preparing his speech.

## Saving Time in Conventions

Since the cost of large conventions is so tremendous, every means should be taken to conserve the time of the convention. There are many ways to do this. The chief responsibility for seeing that things "move along" at a convention rests with the presiding officer. It is his duty to see that the order of business is followed strictly, that motions are proposed promptly, that discussion is confined definitely to the matter before the assembly, that speakers do not exceed their time, and that votes are taken promptly.

Committees can conserve the time of the convention by submitting printed reports. The time frequently devoted to roll calls can be saved by registration on entering or leaving the meeting place. The time consumed by the reading and correction of minutes can be devoted to other matters if a minutes committee is established. The time frequently required by announcements can be cut by requiring that all announcements be written out and handed to an announcement committee. This committee makes all announcements at one time or arranges to have them flashed upon a screen or posted on the bulletin board.

*PART III*
*MOTIONS*

# CHART OF
## MOTIONS CLASSIFIED ACCORDING
### TO THEIR MAIN PURPOSE

## Chapter 22. THE MAIN MOTION

### Purpose

The purpose of a main motion is to bring business before an assembly for its consideration in such a manner that it may be discussed and acted upon.

### Form

PROPOSER: "I move that we hold our Annual Aviation Show on Friday, November second."

*or*

"I move the adoption of the committee report."

*or*

"I move that the appointments of the president be confirmed."

*or*

"I move that the resolution adopted July 28 of last year, providing for a fine of one dollar to be collected from any member who is late at a regular meeting, be repealed."

*or*

"I move that this organization confirm the agreement drawn up by our attorney."

157

*or*

"I move that the Chamber of Commerce of Massachusetts concur in the resolutions drawn up by the Chambers of Commerce of the Atlantic Division, for submission to the national convention."

*or*

"I move that the Executive Committee appoint an assistant controller to aid our Committee on Finance."

*or*

"I move the adoption of the following resolution: 'WHEREAS, The Annual Aviation Show, sponsored by our organization, has been a great success in past years; and

WHEREAS, November second is the most satisfactory date for the show this year; now, therefore, be it *Resolved,* That our organization stage our Annual Aviation Show on Friday, November second; and be it further

*Resolved,* That all organizations in this county be invited to cooperate.' "

or the proposition may be stated simply as follows:

"I move that our Annual Aviation Show be held Friday, November second, and that all organizations in this county be invited to cooperate."

## Explanation

The main motion, since it has so broad a scope, may vary greatly in form. It should be introduced by the words "I move," but otherwise considerable latitude is permitted. It should be as concise and exact as possible and should be stated in the affirmative.

A main motion presents a substantive proposition for decision. It is a formal presentation to an assembly of a subject or question which one of its members desires to have discussed and decided by the organization.[1] A main motion may be, in addition to stating a question in the usual form, a motion to adopt, to ratify, to confirm, to concur, to appoint, to reject, or to repeal.

Main motions may be classified as general and specific. A general main motion is any main motion that presents business for decision by the assembly. Through long use and custom a few main motions have taken on special characteristics and rules and have been given specific names. These are classified as specific main motions. The most frequently used specific main motions are:

1. Reconsider
2. Rescind
3. Resume consideration of a motion
4. Create general or special orders

The specific main motions are subject to most of the rules of a general main motion. These specific main motions are discussed separately under their own names.

## Motions Affecting Actions Already Taken

There are several motions which affect actions already taken. These are the motions to reconsider; to rescind or repeal; to amend a main motion previously adopted; to annul, or void, or cancel; or to repeal by implication, by passing a new measure which conflicts with, overlaps, or is inconsistent with an action already taken.

All of these motions which affect action already taken are main motions and require a majority vote. All these motions can be applied to main motions, and the motion to reconsider can be applied also to amendments and appeals.

The motion to reconsider is discussed in Chapter 23, and the motion to rescind in Chapter 24.

## Effect

The effect of a main motion when proposed is to place business before the assembly. If carried, the effect is to commit the organization to the action stated by the motion.

## Rules Governing a Main Motion

1. Cannot interrupt a speaker because it does not require immediate decision
2. Requires a second to ensure that more than one person is interested in its consideration
3. Is debatable because it presents a substantive proposition for consideration, which is entitled to full and free debate
4. Can be amended to make it express the wishes of the organization
5. Requires a majority vote
6. Has the lowest rank of precedence
7. Applies to no other motion
8. Can have applied to it all subsidiary motions, specific main motions, withdraw, and object to consideration
9. Cannot be renewed at the same meeting or at the same convention. In order to expedite business, it is important that main questions, when once acted upon, are disposed of for the meeting or convention. In order to prevent hasty action in disposing of main questions, reconsideration is permitted, but once the reconsideration is decided, the question cannot be brought up again.

# Chapter 23. MOTION TO RECONSIDER

### Purpose

The purpose of the motion to reconsider is to enable an assembly to set aside a vote previously taken on a motion or resolution and to consider the matter again, as though no vote had been taken.

### Form

PROPOSER [without waiting for recognition]: "I move to reconsider the vote by which the motion to enlarge our library was passed yesterday."

CHAIRMAN (a) [if no other business is pending and after the motion is seconded]: "It has been moved and seconded to reconsider the vote by which the motion to enlarge our library was passed. Is there any discussion? . . . Those in favor of reconsidering the vote by which the motion to enlarge our library was passed say, 'Aye.' . . . Those opposed, 'No.' . . . The motion to reconsider is carried. Therefore, the question of enlarging our library is again open for discussion. Will the secretary please read the motion?"

(b) [if other business is pending]: "It has been moved and seconded to reconsider the vote by which the motion to enlarge our library was passed yesterday. The secretary will please make a note of the motion, and it will be considered as soon as the business now before the assembly has been disposed of."

*Explanation*

1. *What Motions May Be Reconsidered.* The final vote on every main motion, amendment, or appeal may be reconsidered so long as nothing has resulted from the vote which cannot be undone.

It is necessary to give finality to votes on propositions so that the will of the majority may be carried out; otherwise a minority could obstruct the execution of the will of the majority for a long period of time. Therefore, substantive propositions (main motions, amendments, and appeals), once defeated, cannot be renewed and, once approved, cannot be subjected to continuous attack. But lest the action might have been taken inadvertently or without adequate information or in the absence of a large number of members, the vote on substantive propositions is subject for a brief time to reconsideration. The vote on procedural motions may not be reconsidered because the purpose of reconsideration can be accomplished by more simple methods.

Procedural motions that have been lost can be renewed after progress in debate or when there is an essential change in the parliamentary situation.

2. *When Reconsideration Cannot Be Used.* The motion to reconsider is not in order in the following instances:

   *a.* When something has been done as a result of the vote which cannot be undone. For example, when an affirmative vote is in the nature of a contract and the other party to the contract has been notified of the vote[1] or when an officer has been elected and has accepted and qualified for office.[2]

b. When there is an affirmative vote on any rule which requires previous notice for its amendment. For example, a vote on a provision of the constitution or bylaws cannot be reconsidered after their adoption because this would amount to amendment without due notice.

c. When the matter voted upon is out of possession of the assembly, as when a payment, which has been authorized, has been made.

3. *Who May Move to Reconsider*. For many years some parliamentary writers allowed only a member who voted on the prevailing or winning side to propose the motion to reconsider. Theoretically, this limitation on who could propose the motion to reconsider was intended to assure the assembly that at least one member who had a share in deciding the vote had changed his opinion. However, the purpose of this limitation was defeated by the fact that any member of the minority may vote with the majority or may change his vote to the prevailing side before the announcement of the vote and thus gain the right to move to reconsider. Also it is impossible in voice votes to determine how anyone voted. The courts have held that it is not necessary for a member to have voted on the prevailing side in order to move to reconsider unless objection is made, and recent practice avoids this maneuvering to qualify to move to reconsider.

On this point, Cushing said, "Where there is no special rule on this subject, a motion to reconsider may be made . . . by any member, precisely like any other motion, and subject to no other rules."[3]

4. *Time Limit on Moving to Reconsider*. The time during

which a motion to reconsider may be proposed is limited. A motion to reconsider can be made only on the day the vote was taken or on the next business day of a convention. If a convention adjourns from Friday to Monday, a vote taken on Friday may be reconsidered on Monday because that is the next meeting day, but a vote taken at a weekly or monthly meeting cannot be reconsidered at the next weekly or monthly meeting. This rule lends stability to actions of an assembly and allows it to proceed with work which has been authorized by vote.

5. *Proposal of Motion to Reconsider.* The motion to reconsider can be proposed at any time during a meeting, even after a vote to adjourn has been taken but not after adjournment has been announced. It may be proposed even though other business is under consideration. If necessary, it may interrupt a speaker. When the motion to reconsider is proposed while some other business is pending, the secretary records its proposal, but it cannot be considered until the pending business has been disposed of.

6. *Consideration of Motion to Reconsider.* A motion to reconsider, if proposed when no other business is pending, is considered immediately unless its consideration is postponed definitely. A definite postponement of its consideration makes it an order for the time to which it is postponed.

A motion to reconsider, if proposed when other business is pending, is considered as soon as the pending business is disposed of unless its consideration is postponed definitely by majority vote.

7. *Motion to Reconsider and Have Entered on the Minutes.* The motion to reconsider and have entered on the minutes was a device by which two members, one to make the motion and the other to second it, could tie up any business, no matter how urgent, until the next meeting, even though it be months away. It was proposed as a means of preventing

arbitrary action by minorities. The scheme operated by making a motion to reconsider, having it entered on the minutes, and not permitting it to be considered until the next meeting. As a motion to reconsider, it held the action under reconsideration in suspense until the motion was acted upon.

The motion to reconsider and have entered on the minutes has never had general acceptance as a rule of parliamentary law. It exists only when specifically set forth in the bylaws or rules. It is not a rule of parliamentary law.

8. *Debate on Motion to Reconsider.* The motion to reconsider is debatable and opens the main question to be reconsidered to debate. When a member has exhausted his right to debate a question, he may debate the motion again under the motion to reconsider.

9. *Reconsidering Amendments.* When it is desired to reconsider the vote on an amendment after the vote has been taken on the adoption of the main motion, it is necessary to reconsider the vote on the main question and on the amendment. When it is thus necessary to reconsider two or three successive votes, one motion can be made to cover them all.

## Effect

The effect of making the motion to reconsider a vote is to suspend all action on the motion resulting from the vote which it is sought to reconsider until the motion to reconsider is acted upon.

If, however, the motion to reconsider is made and not considered, the effect terminates with the meeting or with the calendar day unless consideration is postponed to a later date.

When a vote is reconsidered, it is canceled as completely as though it had never been taken,[4] and the original motion is again before the assembly as though it had not been voted upon.

## Rules Governing Motion to Reconsider

1. The proposing of the motion to reconsider can interrupt a speaker because the proposing of the motion has a definite time limit
2. Requires a second
3. Is debatable and opens the motion sought to be reconsidered to debate
4. Cannot be amended, since it is a single invariable proposition
5. Requires a majority vote, even though the motion to be reconsidered required a two-thirds vote
6. The motion to reconsider may be proposed at any time within its time limit but its consideration has only the precedence of the motion on which the vote is proposed to be reconsidered
7. Applied to votes on main motions, amendments, and appeals
8. Can have applied to it the motion to withdraw, vote immediately, limit debate, and postpone definitely
9. Cannot be renewed

# Chapter 24. MOTION TO RESCIND

## Purpose

The purpose of the motion to rescind is to nullify or render void a motion previously passed.

## Form

> PROPOSER: "I move to rescind (or repeal, or annul, or cancel, or void) the motion passed June first by which this organization went on record as opposed to the issuance of new school bonds."
>
> CHAIRMAN: "It has been moved and seconded to rescind the motion passed June first, by which this organization went on record as opposed to the issuance of new school bonds. The secretary will please read the motion referred to. . . . Is there any discussion? . . . Those in favor of the motion to rescind this motion, please rise. . . . Those opposed, please rise. . . . The motion is carried. The motion in opposition to the new school bonds is rescinded."

## Explanation

It is important to understand the difference between the motions to reconsider and to rescind. The motion to recon-

167

sider may be made only at the meeting at which the vote to be reconsidered was taken or at the next business day of a convention. The motion to rescind can be made at any time after it is too late to move to reconsider.

Another difference is that the motion to reconsider applies to all substantive motions (main motions, amendments, and appeals), whereas the motion to rescind applies only to main motions.

The motion to rescind is a specific main motion and is in order only whenever there is no business before the assembly.

Motions cannot be rescinded in the following instances:

1. When as a result of the vote something has been done which the assembly cannot undo.[1] For example, if the treasurer is authorized to pay a bill and has done so, it is too late to rescind the authorization.

2. A motion approving a contract when the other party has been informed of the contract and wishes it to continue.

3. A motion electing someone to membership or office if the person was present or has been officially notified of the motion.

The motion to rescind requires a majority vote [2] but an action which requires a majority vote of all members can be rescinded only by a majority vote of all members.[3]

The motion to expunge is often used with the motion to rescind as follows:

"I move to rescind the motion passed on January fifth, relating to . . . and to expunge the record of its passage from the minutes."

If carried, this motion has the effect of officially deleting the expunged motion. When a motion is ordered expunged from the minutes, the secretary does not obliterate the motions but marks it "expunged by order of this assembly" and indicates the date. The expunged record is deleted from any published minutes.

This motion is used only in rare instances where the assembly desires to remove the motion or resolution from its public record.

## Effect

The effect of the motion to rescind, if adopted, is to nullify, repeal, or void the motion rescinded, from the date of the passage of the motion to rescind.

## Rules Governing Motion to Rescind

1. Cannot interrupt a speaker
2. Requires a second
3. Is debatable and opens the question it proposes to rescind to debate
4. Cannot be amended, since it is invariable in form
5. Requires a majority vote
6. Takes precedence as a main motion
7. Applies to main motions previously adopted, except those actions which it is too late to rescind
8. Can have applied to it all subsidiary motions and the motion to withdraw
9. Cannot be renewed at the same meeting or convention

# Chapter 25. RESUME CONSIDERATION

## (TAKE FROM THE TABLE)

### Purpose

The purpose of the motion to resume consideration of a motion (take from the table) which has been postponed temporarily (laid on the table) is to allow the assembly to take up the postponed motion again.

### Form

PROPOSER: "I move to resume consideration of the motion which was postponed temporarily at our last meeting 'that this club undertake a campaign for three hundred new members.'"

*or*

"I move that the motion to . . . be taken from the table."

CHAIRMAN: "It has been moved and seconded that we resume consideration of the motion 'that this club undertake a campaign for three hundred new members.' Those in favor of resuming consideration of the motion say 'Aye.' . . . Opposed, 'No.' . . .

170

The motion is carried, and the motion 'that this club undertake a campaign for three hundred new members' is now open for discussion."

## Explanation

The motion to resume consideration of a matter which has been temporarily postponed is a specific main motion but takes precedence over other main motions. If there is no business before the assembly when a member rises to move to resume consideration and the chairman recognizes someone else, the member should at once state that he rises to move to resume consideration of a motion, and he will be given priority over any other member who wishes to propose a new main motion. If a motion is before the assembly, however, the motion to resume consideration may not be proposed until the business before the assembly is disposed of.

The motion to resume consideration of a question is not in order until some business has been transacted since the motion to postpone the question temporarily was passed.

## Effect

The effect of the motion to resume consideration of a motion, if carried, is to place the original motion before the assembly in exactly the same state as when it was postponed temporarily. Adhering motions are again before the assembly just as they were when the motion was postponed temporarily, except that motions limiting debate lose their effect after the day on which they were adopted.

## Rules Governing Motion to Resume Consideration (Take from the Table)

1. Cannot interrupt a speaker except someone proposing a new main motion
2. Requires a second

3. Is not debatable
4. Cannot be amended
5. Requires a majority vote
6. Has the precedence of a main motion but takes precedence over other new main motions
7. Applies to any question which has been postponed temporarily
8. Can have applied to it no other motions except withdraw
9. Can be renewed after a change in the parliamentary situation

# Chapter 26. CREATE ORDERS

## Purpose

The purpose of the motion to create general or special orders is to fix a definite date or time for the consideration of important motions or to reserve time so that consideration of a subject will be assured.

## Form

> PROPOSER [if the motion to be made an order is not pending]: "I move that the motion [state motion or subject] be made a general order for Friday."
>
> *or*
>
> "I move that the motion [state motion] be made a special order for Friday at three o'clock."
>
> *or*
>
> "I move that the subject of our budget be made a general order for Wednesday evening."
>
> CHAIRMAN: "It has been moved and seconded that the motion [stating motion] be made a general order for Friday's meeting. Is there any discussion? . . .

## Explanation

Orders are motions or subjects which are set for consideration at a particular meeting or hour. They are of two kinds: general orders and special orders. General orders are matters which are set to come up for consideration in the regular order of business at a particular meeting. A majority vote is required to establish a general order. If the motion which was made a general order was a pending motion when it was created an order, it comes up under unfinished business in the regular order of business. If it was not pending when made a general order, it comes up under new business. In either case it has priority over any general business or any other business of its class.

A special order is set for a particular hour. It requires a two-thirds vote to establish because when the hour arrives for which it was set, a special order interrupts any business which is then before the assembly (except another special order), and the special order must be disposed of before the pending business can be resumed.

In case of a conflict between general and special orders, special orders have priority. In case of conflict between orders of the same class, the orders first set prevail over orders later set. When set at the same time, the earlier stated in the motion or resolution setting the order prevails over the later.

Both general and special orders can be created by postponing to a definite time a motion which is pending before the assembly. Creation of orders by the motion to postpone definitely is explained in Chapter 30.

If a motion to create a general or special order is made when no motion is pending, it is a specific main motion. It follows the rules of a main motion except that a special order requires a two-thirds vote and the motion can be amended only as to time and is debatable only as to the propriety of setting the order.

No motion set as a special or general order can be taken

up for consideration before the time set by the order except by a two-thirds vote to suspend the rules.

When the time arrives for considering an order, it can be postponed by a majority vote.

If the presiding officer fails to bring a general or special order before the assembly at the meeting or hour specified for its consideration, any member can bring up the question by rising to a point of order.

## Effect

The effect of the motion to create a general order is to establish a definite place in the order of business of a particular day, for the consideration of the subject of the order.

The effect of the motion to create a special order is to give the subject of the order the right to interrupt all business when the time arrives which was fixed for the consideration of the order.

## Rules Governing Motion to Create Orders (When Motion Is Not Pending)

1. Cannot interrupt a speaker
2. Requires a second
3. Is debatable as to propriety of creating the order but does not open the main motion to debate
4. Can be amended only as to time
5. Requires a majority vote if a general order, a two-thirds vote if a special order
6. Takes precedence as an incidental motion when the question to be made an order is then pending, but if not pending, it takes precedence as a main motion
7. Applies to main motions, including reports
8. Can have only amend and withdraw applied to it
9. Can be renewed after change in the parliamentary situation

# Chapter 27. MOTION TO POSTPONE

## INDEFINITELY

### Purpose

The purpose of the motion to postpone indefinitely is to suppress the question before the assembly, without allowing it to come to a vote. Its purpose is not to postpone, as its name implies, but to reject the main question, without bringing it to a direct vote.

### Form

PROPOSER: "I move that the motion to . . . be postponed indefinitely."

*or*

"I move that consideration [or further consideration] of the resolution be postponed indefinitely."

### Explanation

The motion to postpone indefinitely is a motion to suppress a main motion for the current meeting or convention.

176

The indefinite postponement of a question is equivalent to its complete rejection; it is likewise the equivalent of a negative vote on the main question.[1]

The motion to postpone indefinitely opens the main question to debate, on the principle that any motion which seeks to make final disposition of the main motion opens it to debate. Members who have exhausted their right to debate on the main motion can speak again on the motion to postpone indefinitely since, technically, this motion presents a different question.

Opponents of the main motion sometimes move to postpone it indefinitely in order to learn who is in favor and who is opposed to the main motion, without the risk of adopting it.

## Effect

The effect of the motion to postpone indefinitely, if carried, is to suppress during the meeting or the convention the question to which it applies. It is equivalent to a negative vote on the main motion. A motion which has been indefinitely postponed can be brought up at a later meeting or convention only by proposing it as a new motion.

## Rules Governing Motion to Postpone Indefinitely

1. Cannot interrupt a speaker
2. Requires a second
3. Is debatable because it is equivalent to a negative vote on the main question and disposes finally of the motion It, therefore, opens the main question to debate
4. Cannot be amended because it is invariable in form, and any amendment as to duration of postponement would change it from a motion to suppress the question to one to defer consideration

5. Requires a majority vote
6. Takes precedence of nothing but the main motion
7. Applies to main motions only
8. Can have applied to it only motions to withdraw, to vote immediately, or to limit debate
9. Cannot be renewed

# Chapter 28. MOTION TO AMEND

## Purpose

The purpose of the motion to amend is to modify or change a motion or resolution that is being considered by the assembly so that it will express the will of the assembly more satisfactorily.

## Form

Amendments are of three types. These are amendments:

1. By addition or insertion. This type adds something to the motion which it did not contain originally.
2. By elimination. This type eliminates or strikes out something from the motion which was a part of it originally.
3. By substitution. This type strikes out something and inserts something else as a substitute. The substitution may be a word, a phrase, a clause, or an entirely new motion.

Assume that the following motion is under consideration: "I move that this organization send representatives to the city council and city engineer to present the need for a new park system."

1. *Amendment by addition (insertion)*

    PROPOSER: "I move to insert the word 'three' before the word 'representatives.'"

    CHAIRMAN: "It has been moved and seconded to amend the motion by inserting the word 'three' before the word 'representatives.'" When necessary to a clear understanding, the chairman should also continue: "The motion, if amended, would read, 'that this organization send *three* representatives to the city council and the city engineer to present the need for a new park system.' Is there any discussion? . . . Those in favor of the amendment, which is that the word 'three' be inserted before the word 'representatives,' say 'Aye.' . . . Those opposed, 'No.' . . . The amendment is carried. Is there any discussion upon the motion as amended?"

2. *Amendment by Elimination (Striking Out)*

    PROPOSER: "I move to strike out the words 'and the city engineer.'"

    CHAIRMAN: "It has been moved and seconded to amend the motion by striking out the words, 'and the city engineer,' so that the motion, if amended, would read, 'that this organization send representatives to the city council to present the need for a new park system.'"

3. *Amendment by Substitution (Striking Out and Inserting)*

    a. Substituting words.

    PROPOSER: "I move to amend the motion by striking out the word 'representatives' and inserting in its place the words 'its executive committee.'"

    CHAIRMAN: "It has been moved and seconded to amend the motion by striking out the word 'representatives' and inserting in its place the words 'its

executive committee,' so that the motion, if
amended, would read, 'that this organization send
its executive committee to the city council and city
engineer to present the need for a new park system.'"

b. Substituting a new motion or paragraph.

PROPOSER: "I move to substitute for this motion the
following motion: 'I move that our organization
hold a conference with the city manager to determine how we may cooperate best in securing a new
municipal park system.'"

CHAIRMAN: "It has been moved and seconded to
amend the motion 'that this organization send
representatives to the city council and the city
engineer to present the need for a new park system'
by substituting for it a new motion 'that our organization hold a conference with the city manager to
determine how we may cooperate best in securing
a new municipal park system.'"

*Explanation*

### 1. *What Motions May Be Amended*

The test which determines whether any given motion may
be amended is "Is the motion variable in form?" All motions which may be presented in different forms may be
amended. Motions which may be amended without restric-
tion are:

1. Main motions
2. Amendments

Three motions allow limited amendments as to time only.
These are:

1. Postpone definitely
2. Limit debate
3. Recess

The motion to refer to a committee may be amended as to name, number of members, and method of selection of a committee, or to give instructions to the committee or to otherwise define its work. Requests, demands, and inquiries are not true motions and, therefore, are not subject to amendment.

## 2. Amendments Must Be Germane

The most important principle underlying amendments is that they must be germane. Germane means relevant to, and having direct bearing upon, the subject of the motion which the amendment seeks to change. For example, a motion "that we hold our convention June fourth in Chicago" could be amended by adding the words "and pay the expenses of all delegates" or by adding the words "and that all state adjutants be notified of the date immediately," because both of the amendments relate closely to the main idea of the motion, which is to hold a convention. If, however, an amendment were proposed to add the words "and that we raise the national adjutant's salary," it would not be germane. The chairman should immediately rule this latter amendment out of order by stating: "The chair rules the amendment out of order because it is not germane to the pending motion."

An amendment which would change one form of motion into another form of motion is never in order. For example, if a motion to postpone the pending main motion "until Friday at three o'clock" is before the assembly, and a member moves to amend this motion to postpone definitely by striking out the words "until Friday at three o'clock" and inserting in their place the word "indefinitely," this amendment would be out of order. The proposed amendment would change the motion to postpone definitely to a motion to postpone indefinitely and is therefore not in order.

### 3. *Amendments May Be Hostile*

An amendment may be hostile. That is, it may be opposed to the actual intent of the original motion. It may even nullify the motion. For example, the motion "that we condemn the action of the Committee on Labor in reopening hearings on the Minimum Wage Bill" could be amended by striking out the word "condemn" and inserting the word "endorse." Thus the intent of the original motion would be reversed by a hostile amendment. But this amendment would be germane to the subject matter of the motion, which is an expression of the organization's attitude concerning the action of the committee.

No amendment is in order which merely negates an affirmative motion, as for example, a motion "that we assess members of this local five dollars for the welfare fund" could not be amended to read, "that we do not assess members five dollars for the welfare fund."

### 4. *Limitations on Number of Pending Amendments*

Amendments are of two ranks. Amendments applied to the original motion are amendments of the first rank, and amendments to the proposed amendment are amendments of the second rank.

Only one amendment can be under consideration at a time. When one amendment to a motion is under consideration, another amendment of the same rank is not in order. However, since the amendment may not be satisfactory to the majority of the members, it is necessary that it be possible to amend the amendment before it is adopted. An amendment to an amendment is, therefore, permitted. It is not permissible to propose an amendment to the amendment to the amendment, as this would introduce too much confusion.

Whenever an amendment is adopted or defeated, another amendment of the same rank is in order. Any number of amendments may be offered in succession, provided that only one amendment of each rank is pending at one time. As soon as a pending amendment of the second rank has been disposed of, another of the same rank may be proposed. As soon as the pending amendments of both ranks have been disposed of, another amendment of each rank is in order.

If the motion "that this organization entertain the veterans of Cleveland Hospital next Friday evening" is pending, and someone moves to add the words "at a dinner party at the Wayside Inn," this would be an amendment to the motion. If, when discussion is called for on this amendment, someone proposes an amendment to the amendment to strike out the words "Wayside Inn" and insert the words "Palace Hotel," this would be an amendment to the amendment because it relates directly to the amendment. If, however, someone proposes an amendment to the amendment to strike out the words "Cleveland Hospital" and insert the words "the veterans of all hospitals in the city," this would be ruled out of order because it is an amendment to the original motion, and there is already an amendment of this rank pending.

An amendment to a constitution, bylaws, or any motion which has been previously adopted is a main motion and is, therefore, subject to amendments of both ranks.

## 5. *Debate on Amendments*

When an amendment is proposed, discussion is limited to that amendment until it is disposed of or superseded by an amendment to it. Reference to the main motion is permissible only for the purpose of explaining the amendment or its effect. In discussing an amendment to an amendment, reference to the main motion or to the original amendment is permissible only for the purpose of explaining the amendment to the amendment or its effect.

It is in order, in opposing an amendment, to say that if the amendment is voted down, the speaker will propose another amendment which he may state or describe briefly.

When an amendment is proposed to a motion which is undebatable, the amendment is not debatable.

### 6. *Substituting a New Motion*

When several amendments would be necessary to make a motion acceptable to an assembly, it is better to propose an amendment to substitute a new motion. The substitute may revise the motion completely so long as it is germane to the subject of the original motion.[1]

This proposed substitute amendment is itself subject to an amendment.

### 7. *Filling Blanks*

Resolutions are sometimes presented with blank spaces for filling names, dates, or numbers. These blanks are filled by allowing members who desire, without seconds, to propose names, dates, or numbers to fill the blanks. These are not put to vote in the same manner as amendments. When all suggestions have been offered, the chairman takes the vote beginning with the first proposed, until a date, name, or number receives a majority vote. After the blanks have been filled, a vote must still be taken on the approval of the motion or proposition in which the blanks have been filled.

### 8. *Vote Required*

An amendment to a pending motion requires only a majority vote, even though the motion requires a two-thirds vote. An amendment to any amendment requires only a majority vote.

An amendment to a constitution or bylaws requires a two-thirds vote unless some other vote is specified.

### 9. *Withdrawing Amendments and Accepting Modifications*

The proposer of an amendment may withdraw it by right before it is stated by the presiding officer and may withdraw it at any time with the consent of the assembly.

A member has the right to modify a motion proposed by him at any time before it is stated by the presiding officer, but after it is stated, he can modify it only by unanimous consent or by a motion granting permission to modify the motion.

If the proposer of a motion wishes to accept an amendment which has been offered, he does not need to obtain the floor but says, "Mr. Chairman, I accept the amendment." The chairman asks if there is objection. If no objection is made, the chairman announces that the motion is amended by unanimous consent. If anyone objects, the amendment must be voted upon as a regular amendment.

### 10. *Finality of Amendments*

When an amendment is adopted or when an amendment is rejected, the same, or substantially the same, question or idea cannot be presented again at the same meeting or convention unless the vote originally taken on the amendment is reconsidered. This rule applies whether it is sought to take out an amendment or a part of an amendment previously adopted or to adopt an amendment or a part of an amendment previously rejected or any combination of the two.

This rule is necessary in order to terminate debate upon a question which might otherwise be continued indefinitely by renewing and rephrasing amendments.

Some writers on parliamentary law have sought to solve this problem with a labyrinth of technical rules concerning amendments to insert, strike out, or substitute words, clauses, or paragraphs. These rules fail in their purpose because they can readily be evaded by changes in phraseology. Consideration of the purpose and effect of the amendments will enable the presiding officer to entertain every legitimate amendment and to rule out all amendments when once disposed of.

### Effect

The effect of an amendment, if carried, is to change the original motion or proposition as the amendment provides. The motion or proposition is then considered and voted upon as though it had been originally introduced in the amended form.

### Rules Governing Motion to Amend

1. Cannot interrupt since it does not require immediate decision
2. Requires a second
3. Is debatable, unless applied to an undebatable motion
4. Can be amended
5. Requires a majority vote, even though the motion to which it applies requires a two-third vote
6. Takes precedence only over main motions and the motion to postpone indefinitely
7. Applies to any motion which does not have an invariable form
8. Can have applied to it all subsidiary motions, reconsider and withdraw.
9. Cannot be renewed but may be reconsidered. Amendments when acted upon cannot be changed at the same meeting or convention except by reconsideration of the vote adopting them

## Chapter 29. *MOTION TO REFER TO COMMITTEE*

### Purpose

The purpose of a motion to refer to a committee may be:

1. To secure an investigation of a matter and recommendations on it
2. To ensure privacy when considering a delicate matter
3. To secure consideration by a smaller group so that more thorough and efficient study can be given
4. To permit more informal consideration
5. To delay a proposal or perhaps to defeat it by reference to a hostile committee

### Form

PROPOSER: "I move to refer the motion to a special committee of three to be appointed by the chairman" or "consisting of Mr. A, Mr. B, and Mr. C," or "to a committee to be elected by the assembly," or "to the standing committee on education."

CHAIRMAN [after hearing a second]: "It has been moved

and seconded to refer the motion to a committee consisting of. . . . Is there any discussion on the propriety of referring this question to a committee?"

## Explanation

The proposer of a motion to refer a motion to a committee may include in his motion:

1. The type of committee (special or standing)
2. If a special committee:
   a. Number of members
   b. How members are to be selected
   c. Who is to be chairman
   d. Instructions to the committee

If these details are not included in the motion to refer to a committee, the chairman may settle the points by asking questions of the assembly, such as "How shall this committee be chosen?" These questions may be decided before voting on the motion to refer to a committee or after the motion has carried. Committees to be appointed by the chairman are announced at once, unless the presiding officer needs time to consider the appointments. In this case, he should inform the assembly when the appointments will be made.

Instructions may be given to a committee as a part of the motion to refer a question to a committee, or as an amendment to that motion or as a separate motion. These instructions may be given at any time before the committee submits its final report. A motion to refer to a committee a subject or motion which is not then pending before the assembly is treated as any other main motion. If amendments are pending to the question referred to a committee, the amendments are referred with the question.

If the assembly decides that it wishes to dispose of the question in some other manner, it may withdraw the question from the committee at any time.

### Effect

The effect of the motion to refer to a committee, if carried, is to transfer the referred subject to the committee immediately. If any amendment to the referred motion is pending, it goes to the committee with the motion. A motion to refer an amendment to a committee takes with it the motion to which the amendment applies.

### Rules Governing Motion to Refer to Committee

1. Cannot interrupt a speaker because it does not require immediate decision
2. Requires a second
3. Is open to debate only on the propriety of referring the question to a committee. A motion giving instructions to the committee is open to discussion on the instructions.
4. Can be amended as to:
   a. Type or number of committee
   b. Method of selection
   c. Who is to be chairman
   d. Instructions to the committee
5. Requires a majority vote
6. Takes precedence of the motion to amend and postpone indefinitely
7. Can be applied to main motions or amendments
8. Can have applied to it only the motion to amend, the motions to close or limit debate and withdraw
9. Can be renewed after change in the parliamentary situation

# Chapter 30. MOTION TO POSTPONE

## DEFINITELY

## Purpose

The purpose of the motion to postpone definitely, or to a certain time, is to postpone consideration of a motion to a later time and to fix a time for consideration, or for further consideration, of the motion. It is quite different in effect from the motion to postpone indefinitely, which seeks to suppress the main motion, or from the motion to postpone temporarily, which seeks to set aside a question until a more convenient, but still undetermined, time.

The motion to postpone definitely provides a satisfactory and convenient means of fixing in advance the day or the time when a question will come up for consideration and makes the question postponed an order for that day or time.

## Form

PROPOSER: "I move to postpone consideration of the motion until the next meeting" or "until Friday at three o'clock" or "until after the installation of officers at this evening's meeting."

CHAIRMAN: "It has been moved and seconded that [stating the motion] be postponed until the next meeting. Is there any discussion on the propriety of postponing this question to the next meeting?"

## Explanation

The motion to postpone definitely cannot be used so that its effect would be substantially the same as a motion to postpone indefinitely. The following limitations are therefore placed upon the motion to postpone definitely:

1. It is not permissible to postpone a question beyond the next regular meeting or the end of the convention or to any time when it would be too late to act upon the question.

2. No amendment is in order which would convert a motion to postpone definitely into a motion to postpone indefinitely.

3. A question may not be postponed to a special or adjourned meeting until the meeting has been provided for.

When a motion or subject is postponed to a definite day or hour, it becomes a general order for that day or hour. When the time comes for the consideration of a general order, it does not interrupt the question under consideration at that hour but should be taken up as soon as the question under consideration is disposed of. If a motion is not set for that particular hour, it comes up under "orders" in the order of business, or if orders are not listed, it comes up under "unfinished business." Orders are explained in Chapter 26.

If a subject or motion is set as a special order for a particular time, it interrupts any business pending at that time. When the time arrives for its consideration, it is the duty of the presiding officer to interrupt anyone who has the floor and to state the special order. Because of this right of a special order to interrupt any pending business, a two-thirds vote is required to set any special order.

No motion which has been postponed to a definite time can be taken up before that time except by a motion to suspend the rules. No class of business, such as committee reports, may be postponed as a whole but may be postponed by a vote on each separate item.

When the bylaws or standing rules set a definite time for considering a matter, it cannot be postponed until that time arrives. For example, if a nominating committee's report is set for a certain meeting and weather conditions make a representative meeting impossible, the report can be postponed when the meeting convenes but not beforehand. If a matter which was postponed is not taken up at the time set, it becomes unfinished business.

## Effect

The effect of the motion to postpone definitely is to make the matter postponed a general order for the meeting to which it was postponed. If set by a two-thirds vote for a particular hour, the matter becomes a special order.

## Rules Governing Motion to Postpone Definitely

1. Cannot interrupt a speaker since the motion does not require immediate consideration
2. Requires a second
3. Open to restricted debate on the propriety of postponing the particular question to the particular time. It does not open the main question to debate
4. Can be amended only as to the time of postponement since that is the only variable portion of the motion
5. Requires a majority vote
6. Takes precedence of the motion to refer to committee, to amend, and to postpone indefinitely

7. Applies to main motions only
8. Can have applied to it only the motions regulating debate, amendments as to time, and withdraw
9. Can be renewed after a change in the parliamentary situation

## Chapter 31. LIMIT OR EXTEND LIMITS

## OF DEBATE

### Purpose

The purpose of the motion to limit debate is to restrict the length of time which will be devoted to discussion. The purpose of the motion to extend the limits of debate is to modify or remove restrictions already imposed in order to increase the time allotted to debate.

### Form

PROPOSER: "I move to limit the time of each speaker on this question to three minutes."

*or*

"I move to limit debate on this question to four speeches in favor and four speeches against."

*or*

"I move to limit debate on the motion to two hours."

*or*

"I move that the time of the speaker be extended twenty minutes."

### Explanation

The motion to limit debate is usually made in one of the

four forms suggested in the previous paragraph. However, there is a wide latitude in the forms which may be used to meet the particular situation. If one form of the motion to limit debate has been proposed and is pending before the assembly, another form of the motion limiting debate that does not conflict with the first may be moved as an amendment; for example, if the motion "to limit each speaker to five minutes" is pending, an amendment may be proposed to add "and limit the number of speakers to six" or "to limit the time for debate to one hour."

If the proposer of the motion does not specify upon what motion he desires the discussion limited, only the immediately pending question is affected.

The motion to extend the limits of debate is subject to the same rules and conditions as the motion to limit debate. The most common form is the motion to extend the time allowed a particular speaker.

A motion modifying the limits of debate either by curtailing or extending them is in force only during the meeting or convention at which it was adopted. If the main motion is postponed until another meeting, the order limiting debate loses its force.

Both the motion to limit debate and the motion to extend the limits of debate are frequently approved by unanimous consent.

### Effect

The effect of the motion to limit debate is to cut down the total time devoted to discussion of a motion, the length of speeches or their number, or otherwise to limit or restrict debate. The effect of a motion to extend the limits of debate is to allow more time for debate or to remove limits or restrictions.

*Rules Governing Motions Limiting or Extending Limits of Debate*

1. Cannot interrupt a speaker since it does not require immediate decision
2. Requires a second
3. Is not debatable
4. Can be amended only as to time for debate, length of speeches, number of speakers, or other similar changes
5. Requires two-thirds vote since a motion to limit debate infringes on the principle of full and free discussion, and a motion to extend debate sets aside an already established limit on debate
6. Takes precedence of the motions to postpone definitely, refer to a commitee, amend, and postpone indefinitely
7. Applies to all debatable questions
8. Can have applied to it only motions to amend and withdraw
9. Can be renewed after change in the parliamentary situation or progress in debate

# Chapter 32. MOTION TO VOTE IMMEDIATELY

## (PREVIOUS QUESTION)

### Purpose

The purpose of the motion to vote immediately is to prevent or to stop all discussion on the question or questions before the assembly, to prevent the proposal of subsidiary motions, and to bring the question or questions to vote immediately.

### Form

> PROPOSER: "I move that we vote immediately on the motion to . . ."
>
> or
>
> "I move to vote immediately on all pending questions before the assembly [or on the amendments, etc.]."
>
> or
>
> if preferred, the old form may be used:
> "I move the previous question."
>
> CHAIRMAN: "It has been moved and seconded to vote immediately on the motion before the assembly.

Those in favor of voting immediately, please rise.
. . . Be seated. Those opposed, please rise. . . . Be
seated. There being a two-thirds vote in the affirmative, the motion to vote immediately is carried. We
will now vote on the main motion."

The old form for putting the "previous question" to vote
was, "Shall the main question be now put?"

## Explanation

The proper use and form of the motion, which was known
as the "previous question," has been a problem since the
time of Thomas Jefferson. According to him, it was introduced in Parliament in 1604 and was originally a debatable motion to suppress motions of "a delicate nature as
to high personages and so forth," and it was his opinion that
"its uses would be as well answered by other more simple
parliamentary forms."

The "previous question" has so changed in use in America
that the old English name and form is entirely misleading,
and in common practice the name "previous question" has
been superseded by the more simple parliamentary terms
"vote immediately" or "close debate." The motion to vote
immediately is more than a motion to close debate, however,
since it also prevents the proposal of subsidiary motions and
brings the question or questions to which it is applied to vote
immediately. The term "vote immediately" is, therefore,
more accurate and descriptive.

The motion to vote immediately is used to prevent debate
and to prevent the proposal of subsidiary motions, or it is
used to close debate which is already in progress or to prevent the making of some other subsidiary motion or both.

If the motion to vote immediately is stated without any
qualification, it applies only to the question immediately
pending. The motion may be qualified to make it apply to

successive pending motions. If the motion to vote immediately is qualified to make it apply to all pending questions, its effect continues until the main motion before the assembly is decided. For example, if a main motion, an amendment, and a motion to refer to a committee are pending, and the motion to vote immediately is carried, it applies only to the motion to refer to a committee, and that motion must be voted upon at once. If, in the same situation, the motion "to vote immediately on everything before the assembly" is carried, an immediate vote must be taken on the motion to refer to a committee. If this motion is lost, a vote is then taken immediately on the amendment and on the main motion.

The effect of the motion to vote immediately terminates with the meeting at which it is adopted. For example, if after the motion to vote immediately has carried, the assembly votes to postpone the main question temporarily and then resumes consideration of the same main question later at the same meeting, the motion to vote immediately still applies and no debate is permitted. However, if consideration of the same main question is not resumed until a later meeting, the effect of the motion to vote immediately has terminated and the main question is again open to debate.

The motion to vote immediately is the most drastic of the motions which seek to control debate, and its object is contrary to the fundamental principle that questions should be decided only after full and free discussion. A two-thirds vote is, therefore, necessary to order an immediate vote.

## Effect

The effect of the motion to vote immediately, if proposed before discussion has started, is to prevent discussion and to prevent the making of subsidiary motions and to bring the motion or motions to which it is applied to an immediate vote. If debate is already in progress, the motion to vote immediately cuts off debate and subsidiary motions and brings the motion or motions to which it is applied to an immediate vote.

## Rules Governing Motion to Vote Immediately (Previous Question)

1. Cannot interrupt a speaker, since it does not require immediate decision
2. Requires a second
3. Is not debatable, since its object, which is to shut off debate, would be defeated
4. Cannot be amended but it may be qualified or limited as to its application by the proposer
5. Requires a two-thirds vote because it sets aside the fundamental principle that decisions on questions should be arrived at after full and free debate [1]
6. Takes precedence over all subsidiary motions except postpone temporarily
7. Applies to any debatable question
8. Can have no motions applied to it except withdraw
9. Can be renewed after change in the parliamentary situation

# Chapter 33. POSTPONE TEMPORARILY

## (LAY ON THE TABLE)

### Purpose

The purpose of the motion to postpone temporarily (lay on the table) is to set aside the consideration of a motion until a later but undetermined time. It provides a means of deferring consideration of a matter temporarily, without prejudice, and allows it to be considered again in preference to any other new motion, whenever the assembly wishes.

### Form

> PROPOSER: "I move that the motion [or the appeal or the amendment] be postponed temporarily."
> *or if preferred, the old form of the motion may be used:*
> "I move that the motion [or amendment] be laid on the table."

### Explanation

Frequently an assembly wishes to temporarily put aside a question without discussing it or, after some discussion, to defer further discussion and decision until another time. There are several reasons why this may be desirable. Some more urgent business may arise, the opponents of a motion may wish to put it aside without permitting debate, the proponents of the motion may feel doubtful of their chance to carry the motion and wish time to win more votes, or the assembly may wish additional information before voting on the motion.

A motion to postpone temporarily defers the question until such time as the assembly decides to resume its consideration. The assembly brings the matter before it again by the motion to resume consideration of the motion, or if the old form of the motion is used, by the motion "to take from the table."

The early form of the motion to "lay on the table" grew out of the custom, in legislative bodies, of laying a bill on the clerk's table for future consideration. In common parliamentary practice both forms are used, but the term "postpone temporarily" is clear and self-explanatory, whereas the term "lay on the table" is often confusing.

A motion which is postponed temporarily is postponed to a time as yet undetermined. To specify any definite time would change the motion to a motion to postpone definitely.

If a main motion is postponed temporarily, all pending amendments and other adhering motions are postponed with it. Likewise, if an amendment is pending and a motion carries to postpone the amendment temporarily, the main motion is postponed with it.

Since it is impossible to apply the motion to any question not before the assembly, an entire class of business, such as unfinished business or committee reports, cannot be postponed temporarily as a whole.

*Effect*

The effect of a motion to postpone temporarily is to stop debate and to remove the motion which is postponed and all amendments and other adhering motions from the consideration of the assembly until the subject is reopened by a motion to resume consideration.

*Rules Governing Motion to Postpone Temporarily (Lay on the Table)*

1.  Cannot interrupt a speaker
2.  Requires a second
3.  Is not debatable because its object is to postpone debate
4.  Cannot be amended because it is invariable in form
5.  Requires a majority vote
6.  Takes precedence over all other subsidiary motions
7.  Applies to main motions, amendments, and appeals
8.  Can have no other motions applied to it except withdraw
9.  Can be renewed after change in the parliamentary situation

## Chapter 34. APPEAL

### Purpose

The purpose of an appeal from a decision of the chair is to enable a member who feels that the presiding officer has made a mistake or has been unfair in his decision to have the assembly decide by vote whether the chairman's decision should be upheld or overruled.

### Form

> PROPOSER [immediately following the chairman's decision and without waiting for recognition]: "Mr. Chairman, I appeal from the decision of the chair."
>
> CHAIRMAN: "The decision of the chair has been appealed from. Will the member appealing please state his grounds for appeal?"

The chairman may state the reasons for his decision either before or after giving an opportunity for discussion. The question may be put to vote by saying:

"Those in favor of sustaining the decision of the chair say, 'Aye.' . . . Those opposed, 'No.' . . . The decision of the chair is sustained [or overruled]."

## Explanation

An appeal is the means by which an assembly may review the decisions of its presiding officer.[1] Any decision of the chairman is subject to appeal. An answer to a parliamentary inquiry or the announcement of a vote is not a decision and cannot be appealed.

An appeal can be taken only immediately after the decision has been rendered. If any other business has intervened or progress has been made in debate, an appeal is not in order. If a member has secured the floor for some other purpose, he may be interrupted by an appeal if it is taken promptly.

An appeal is debatable. Some earlier parliamentary writers held that appeals on misconduct and priority of business could not be debated, but the established practice is to permit all appeals to be discussed before the vote is taken. The chairman may, without leaving the chair, state the reasons for his decision.

If the member's statement of his reasons for appeal proves to the chairman that the decision was incorrect, the chairman himself may reverse his decision, whereupon the appeal is automatically dropped.

Some legislative bodies allow an appeal to be killed by postponing it temporarily (laying it on the table) and not permitting it to be taken up again. In ordinary assemblies this procedure is not used and a direct vote of the assembly is the only way to finally dispose of an appeal.

The presiding officer's decision on an appeal is sustained by a majority vote or by a tie vote. A tie vote sustains the chairman's decision because a majority vote is necessary to overrule his decision. The presiding officer, if a member, may vote to sustain his own decision.

## Effect

The effect of making an appeal is to refer a ruling by the presiding officer to the assembly for its approval or rejection. If the chairman is sustained, his decision becomes the decision of the assembly. If the chairman is not sustained, his decision is overruled.

Rulings by the presiding officer on points of order and decisions of the assembly on appeals are an important source of precedents by which parliamentary law is developed.

## Rules Governing Appeal

1. Can interrupt a speaker because it may require immediate decision and it has a time limit on its presentation
2. Requires a second, since it is equivalent to a motion to overrule the decision of the presiding officer
3. Is debatable
4. Cannot be amended, since an appeal is invariable in form
5. Requires a majority or tie vote to sustain the chairman's decision
6. Takes precedence as an incidental motion over all motions except privileged motions
7. Applies to no motions, but applies to any decision of the presiding officer
8. Can have applied to it the motions to postpone temporarily, postpone definitely, vote immediately, limit debate, withdraw, and reconsider
9. Cannot be renewed

# Chapter 35. POINTS OF ORDER

*Purpose*

The purpose of a point of order is to call attention to a violation of the rules or to an omission or to a mistake in procedure.

It may be used to insist on strict compliance with the rules or to raise a question concerning the interpretation or application of the rules.

*Form*

> PROPOSER [without waiting for recognition]: "Mr. Chairman, I rise to a point of order."
>
> CHAIRMAN [without waiting for a second]: "State your point of order."
>
> PROPOSER: "My point of order is that the motion just proposed is out of order because there is another main motion before the assembly."
>
> CHAIRMAN: "Your point of order is well taken. The motion last proposed is out of order."
>
> or
>
> "Your point of order is not well taken. There is no other main motion pending. The speaker [meaning the member who had the floor before the interruption] may continue."

*Explanation*

It is the duty of the presiding officer to enforce all rules of the assembly and of parliamentary procedure. It is the right of every member who notices a violation of a rule to insist on its enforcement.

A point of order must be raised immediately after the mistake, error, or omission occurs. It cannot be brought up later unless the error involves a violation of the law or of the constitution or bylaws. It is never too late to correct a violation of the law or of the constitution or bylaws.

The raising of a point of order is equivalent to a demand that the presiding officer give a ruling or decision on the point which the member raises.

Since it is important that no business should proceed until a mistake has been corrected, a point of order may be raised at any time, even though a speaker has the floor. The member rising states that he is rising to a point of order so that the chairman may know that he is entitled to recognition. As soon as the member has stated the point of order, the chairman must "rule" on it; that is, give a decision upon the point of order, stating the reasons for his decision if he desires.

An appeal may always be taken from the decision of the chairman.

If the presiding officer is in doubt, or does not wish to assume the responsibility for making the decision, he may consult the parliamentarian or others, or he may refer the matter to the assembly for a decision in the following manner:

"Mr. A has raised the point of order that the amendment just proposed is the same as an amendment already defeated. The chairman is in doubt and refers the matter to the assembly. The question is: 'Is this amendment [stating it] the same as the amendment defeated earlier this evening [stating it]?' Those who believe that it is the same say, 'Aye.' . . . Those who believe that it is not the same, 'No.' The decision is in the affirmative; the amendment, therefore, is declared out of order."

If the chairman wishes, he may refer the point of order to the assembly and call for discussion. Discussion, however, cannot take place unless it is called for by the presiding officer or unless an appeal is taken. If a member wishes to debate or challenge a decision on a point of order, he must first appeal the decision.

When a point of order raises a question which is particularly complicated or is very important and the chairman does not know what ruling to make, he may state that his decision will be deferred until he has had opportunity to do research and to examine precedents. When the decision on a point of order is thus deferred, action on the matter affected by the point of order is likewise deferred.

## Effect

The effect of raising a point of order is to stop all proceedings until the point of order has been decided. If the point of order is held to be "well taken," the chairman orders the mistake corrected. If the point of order is held to be "not well taken," business is resumed at the point where it was interrupted.

## Rules Governing Point of Order

1. Can interrupt a speaker because a mistake should be corrected immediately
2. Requires no second because it is a question or demand and not a true motion
3. Is not debatable unless the presiding officer refers it to the assembly for debate

4. Cannot be amended, since it is a demand or request and not a true motion
5. Requires no vote, since it is not a motion
6. Takes precedence as an incidental motion over all motions except privileged motions
7. Applies to any mistake, error, or omission
8. Can have no motions applied to it except withdraw. The decision on the point of order may be appealed
9. Cannot be renewed

# Chapter 36. PARLIAMENTARY INQUIRY

## Purpose

The purpose of a parliamentary inquiry is to enable a member to obtain information from the presiding officer concerning some question of procedure relating to the motion pending before the assembly or which may be brought before the assembly immediately. A request for information concerning the pending question and a request to ask the speaker a question are variations of a parliamentary inquiry.

## Form

1. *Parliamentary Inquiry*

    PROPOSER [without waiting for recognition]: "I rise to a parliamentary inquiry."

    CHAIRMAN [without waiting for a second]: "State your inquiry."

    PROPOSER: "Is an amendment in order at this time?"

    CHAIRMAN: "It is."

2. *Request for Information*

    PROPOSER [without waiting for recognition]: "I rise to a parliamentary inquiry."

CHAIRMAN [without waiting for a second]: "State your inquiry."

PROPOSER: "I should like to know whether this proposed motion has been approved by the national board of our organization."

CHAIRMAN: "It has already been approved."

3. *Leave to Ask a Question*

PROPOSER [without waiting for recognition]: "I should like to ask the speaker a question."

CHAIRMAN: "Is the speaker willing to yield to a question?"

SPEAKER: "I will yield" or "I will answer questions later" or "I do not care to yield."

## Explanation

A parliamentary inquiry is technically a request rather than a motion. Any member has the right at any time to know what question is being considered and what its effect will be. He also has the right to ask for information concerning motions which are before the assembly or procedure which may be in order.

A parliamentary inquiry or request for information or a question asked of a speaker, if requiring an immediate answer, may interrupt a speaker. No member should interrupt a speaker with an inquiry if it can wait until the speech is concluded. In order that the presiding officer may know that the member rising to a parliamentary inquiry has a right to the floor, the member should state the purpose for which he rises without waiting for recognition.

A parliamentary inquiry is always addressed to and answered by the presiding officer. If the chairman is in doubt, he may consult the parliamentarian or members before answering. A question asked of a speaker is always addressed as a request to the chairman, who asks the speaker if he is willing to allow the question to be stated. If the speaker consents, the question is addressed to the chairman, who then inquires if the speaker will answer it. The answer is directed to the presiding officer and no direct interchange of discussion between questioner and speaker is allowed. The speaker, after hearing the question, may decline to answer it.

If a speaker is interrupted by a parliamentary inquiry and the presiding officer decides that the question does not necessitate an immediate answer, he replies that he will answer the inquiry as soon as the speaker has finished and directs the speaker to continue his discussion. The chairman should never allow a parliamentary inquiry to be used as a method of annoying the speaker who has the floor, and he should refuse recognition to any member who rises repeatedly.

The presiding officer should, when requested by a member, answer any question on parliamentary law which is pertinent to the pending business in order to enable a member to raise a timely point of order or to make a suitable motion. It is not his duty, however, to answer general questions on parliamentary law which are not related to the pending business.

### Effect

The effect of a parliamentary inquiry is to interrupt all business until the chairman answers or declines to answer the inquiry.

### Rules Governing Parliamentary Inquiry

1. Can interrupt a speaker because it may necessitate an immediate answer
2. Requires no second because it is a request and not a true motion

3. Is not debatable because it is a request which is decided by the chairman
4. Cannot be amended
5. Requires no vote because it is decided by the chairman
6. Takes precedence as an incidental motion over all motions except privileged motions
7. Applies to no other motion
8. Can have no motion applied to it except withdraw
9. Cannot be renewed

# Chapter 37. WITHDRAW A MOTION

## Purpose

The purpose of withdrawing a motion is to enable a member to remove from the consideration of the assembly a motion which he has proposed.

## Form

> PROPOSER [of the original motion, after receiving recognition]: "I ask leave to withdraw my motion."
>
> *or*
>
> "I wish to withdraw my motion."
>
> CHAIRMAN [without waiting for a second]: "Mr. B asks leave to withdraw his motion. If there is no objection, the motion will be withdrawn." [Hesitating, to permit objection] "There being no objection, the motion is withdrawn."

If any member objects, the presiding officer may put the question to vote, or the proposer or any other member, after obtaining recognition, may present the following motion:

"I move that permission be granted to withdraw the motion."

## Explanation

Before a motion has been stated by the chairman, its proposer is allowed to modify or withdraw it at his pleasure. If he desires to withdraw it, he says, "I withdraw my motion."

Once the motion has been stated to the assembly, however, it becomes the property of that body, and the proposer may withdraw it only if no objection is raised or if he is given permission by a majority vote.

Until the motion is stated to the assembly, any member or the presiding officer may request the mover to withdraw his motion. Usually this request is made because some more urgent business needs prior consideration. If the proposer declines to withdraw his motion, the chairman proceeds as though no request had been made.

When a motion has been stated to the assembly and the mover requests permission to withdraw his motion, the chairman asks if there is objection, and if there is none, he announces that the motion is withdrawn. If anyone objects to the withdrawal of the motion, it is necessary either for the chairman to take a vote upon the request on his own initiative or for the proposer or some other member to present a motion granting leave to withdraw. A motion can be withdrawn up to the moment the final vote upon the motion is taken, even though other motions affecting it may be pending or debate has been limited or closed.

Any motion can be withdrawn.

## Effect

The effect of withdrawing a motion which has not been stated by the chairman is to take it from the consideration of the assembly as though it had never been proposed. No mention need be made of such a motion in the minutes. When the motion has been stated by the chairman, the effect is to remove the motion from the consideration of the assembly unless objection is made, in which case a motion giving permission to withdraw it is necessary. When permission has been granted to withdraw a motion, the effect is the same as though the motion had not been proposed. When a motion is withdrawn, all secondary motions adhering to it are likewise withdrawn.

*Rules Governing Request to Withdraw a Motion*

1. Cannot interrupt a speaker because it does not require immediate decision
2. Requires no second because it is a request
3. Is not debatable
4. Cannot be amended because it is invariable in form
5. Is not put to vote because it is a request—granted by unanimous consent or defeated by an objection
6. Takes precedence as an incidental motion over all motions except privileged motions
7. Applies to any motion
8. May have no motion applied to it
9. May be renewed after change in the parliamentary situation

The motion granting leave to withdraw a motion follows the same rules as the request except that, being a motion, it requires a second and a majority vote.

# Chapter 38. MOTION TO SUSPEND RULES

## Purpose

The purpose of the motion to suspend rules is to allow an assembly to take some action which it is prevented from taking by the rules of parliamentary procedure, by a program already adopted, or by a standing rule.

## Form

PROPOSER: "I move to suspend the rules which interfere with [state proposed action]."

CHAIRMAN: "It has been moved and seconded to suspend the rules which interfere with. . . . Those in favor, please rise. . . . Be seated. Those opposed, please rise. . . . Be seated. The vote is affirmative, 92. Negative, 18. The rules are suspended. We will proceed with the consideration of. . . ."

## Explanation

When an organization desires to accomplish a specific purpose which it is prevented from doing by the rules of procedure, by an adopted program, or by the standing rules, it is possible to suspend the rules which interfere with the accomplishment of this purpose.[1]

Examples of the use of this motion might occur as follows:

1. When a convention has already adopted a program fixing definite times for speakers and a guest arrives whom the members desire to hear speak, a suspension of the program rules interfering with hearing the guest speaker would enable the assembly to hear him.
2. When a standing rule states that all members who come late shall pay a fine and a traffic tie-up prevents members from being prompt, a suspension of the rule for fines for that particular meeting would be in order.

The motion to suspend rules may be made when no question is pending, or it may be made while a question is pending if it is for a purpose connected with that motion. Rules to which this motion most often applies are those relating to priority of business or to business procedure or procedural rules.

Rules may be suspended only for a limited purpose and for a limited time. Any suspension designed to be effective for a longer period would be an amendment to the rules and not a suspension. For this reason, the object of the suspension must be specified, and nothing which was not mentioned in the motion to suspend the rules can be done under the suspension.

## Effect

The effect of the motion to suspend rules, if carried, is to enable the assembly to take the action which the rules prevented. A suspended rule becomes effective again as soon as the purpose for which it was suspended has been accomplished.

*Rules Governing Motion to Supend Rules*

1. Cannot interrupt a speaker, since it does not require immediate decision
2. Requires a second
3. Is not debatable
4. Cannot be amended because it is invariable in form
5. Requires a two-thirds vote because it sets aside rules of the assembly or rules of procedure
6. Takes precedence as an incidental motion over all motions except privileged motions
7. Applies to no other motions
8. Can have no motion except the motion to withdraw applied to it
9. May be renewed after change in the parliamentary situation

# Chapter 39. OBJECTION TO CONSIDERATION

## Purpose

The purpose of objection to consideration is to avoid entirely the discussion of any question which the assembly believes to be embarrassing, contentious, or unprofitable, or which, for any reason, it does not wish to consider. It may also be used to prevent discussion of a motion which may be presented at an inopportune time.

## Form

PROPOSER [without waiting for recognition]: "Mr. Chairman, I object to the consideration of this question."

CHAIRMAN [without waiting for a second]: "Objection has been raised to the consideration of this question. All in favor of considering the question, please rise. . . . Be seated. Those opposed, please rise. . . . Be seated. There being a two-thirds vote in the negative, the objection is sustained, and the question will not be considered."

*or*

"Since the objection has failed to receive a two-thirds vote in the negative, the objection is not sustained, and the question will now be considered."

## Explanation

Objection to consideration applies only to main motions and to communications except those from a superior body. The following is an example of the use of objection to consideration: In a meeting of a local chapter of a national organization, a motion is proposed "that the annual contribution of each chapter to the national association be changed from two dollars per capita to one dollar per capita." Some member might properly object to the consideration of this motion on the ground that such a change in national policy could only be made by the national association.

Objection to consideration does not apply to amendments to the constitution or bylaws or to reports of committees or to communications from a superior body.

Objection to consideration must be raised as soon as the motion has been stated by the chairman. After substantial progress in debate or some other motion has been applied to the main motion, it is no longer possible to object to its consideration.

Whenever objection to consideration is made, the chairman immediately puts the question of consideration to vote. A two-thirds vote against consideration is required to sustain the objection because, ordinarily, any member of an organization has a right to present a proposal and have it considered. The vote should be taken by a rising vote in order to establish readily whether there is a two-thirds vote in the negative.

If a motion is obviously completely unsuitable for consideration or is proposed to heckle, delay, or embarrass or is tactless, foolish, or unnecessary, the chairman may rule the motion out of order on his own initiative, or if objection is raised, he may rule it out without putting the objection to vote.

## Effect

The effect of an objection to consideration is to shut off all debate on the main motion until the objection is put to vote. If the objection carries, the motion objected to cannot be brought up again at the same meeting or convention except by unanimous consent or by a suspension of the rules.

## Rules Governing Objection to Consideration

1. Can interrupt a speaker because the objection must be raised before progress in debate
2. Requires no second because it is an objection and not a true motion
3. Is not debatable, since its purpose is to avoid all debate on the question
4. Cannot be amended because it is invariable in form
5. Requires a two-thirds negative vote to prevent the consideration of a motion because it sets aside the fundamental right of members to have consideration given to motions which they introduce
6. Takes precedence as an incidental motion over all motions except privileged motions
7. Applies to main motions only
8. Can have no other motions applied to it except withdraw
9. Cannot be renewed because it can be raised only immediately following the presentation of the main motion

# Chapter 40. DIVISION OF A QUESTION

## Purpose

The purpose of a demand for division of a question is to enable the assembly to divide a motion which is composed of two or more independent parts or ideas into individual motions, which may be considered and voted upon separately. It enables a member to insist upon separate votes on independent questions and thus prevent "logrolling," by combining independent proposals in a single motion.

## Form

Assume that the following motion has been proposed:

"I move that the annual meeting be postponed one month and that the dues be increased from five dollars to ten dollars."

PROPOSER [without waiting for recognition and even though a speaker has the floor]: "I request [or demand] that the motion be divided into a motion to postpone the annual meeting for one month and a motion to increase the dues from five dollars to ten dollars."

CHAIRMAN [without waiting for a second, if in his opinion the question contains more than one distinct proposal]: "It is requested [or demanded] that the motion be divided into two parts. This will be done. The motion now before the assembly is that the annual meeting be postponed one month."

## Explanation

### 1. *Right to Demand Division*

When a question contains two or more separate and distinct propositions, each of which is capable of standing alone as a reasonable proposition that could have been offered independently of the others, then it is the right of any member to demand that the question be divided into separate motions.

A member may demand a division in the following instances:

1. When a motion contains more than one independent proposition
2. When a group of amendments cover different points
3. When a committee report contains a number of recommendations

### 2. *What Questions May Not Be Divided*

The presiding officer has the decision as to whether or not a question can be divided. He is governed by the following principles:

1. To be divisible, a question must be composed of propositions each of which is so separate and distinct that one or more are suitable for adoption even if all the others were rejected.
2. If a motion contains only one subject, no matter how complicated it may be, it cannot be divided on a request but must be divided by a definite motion. The motion to divide is not in order if it proposes a division in which any one of the propositions would be absurd

if adopted alone. For example, a motion "that the club erect a headquarters building and rent the extra floors to other tenants" could not be divided because the proposal to rent to other tenants would be meaningless if the proposal to build a headquarters failed.

3. When a motion contains several propositions so arranged that they cannot be divided without rewriting them, a motion to divide the motion is necessary.

4. A request or demand to divide a motion must not require the secretary to do more than separate the proposition into the proposed parts and preface each part with the words "I move" or "Resolved" and make the necessary changes in grammar. If a motion cannot be divided by the assembly, it may be amended or may be referred to a committee with instructions to clarify or divide it.

3. *Motion to Divide a Question*

The motion must state clearly just how the question is to be divided, and it is the privilege of any member to propose a different division. These different proposed motions are alternative propositions, not amendments, and should be voted on in the order in which they are proposed.

The motion or the request to divide a question may be made at any time when the question requires division. It should be proposed immediately after the introduction of the motion which it seeks to divide but it may be proposed even after the question to postpone indefinitely or to vote immediately is pending. The formality of a vote on dividing a question is generally dispensed with and the division is agreed to by general consent. If there is any objection, however, a formal vote to divide is necessary.

*Effect*

The effect of a demand for division of a question is to

cause the presiding officer to rule upon whether the motion
or resolution or amendment can be divided. If he decides
that the motion can be divided, he states the first portion of
the motion and calls for discussion upon it. The effect of a
motion for division of a question, if carried, is to cause the
presiding officer to divide the question as voted and to state
the first part immediately to the organization for its consideration.

*Rules Governing a Demand for a Division of a Question*

1. Cannot interrupt a speaker
2. Requires no second, as it is a demand rather than a
   motion
3. Is not debatable
4. Cannot be amended
5. Requires no vote because it is decided by the chairman
6. Takes precedence as an incidental motion over all
   motions except privileged motions
7. Applies to main motions, amendments, and committee
   recommendations
8. Can have no motions applied to it except withdraw
9. Cannot be renewed

The motion to divide a motion follows the same rules as a
motion to amend.

# Chapter 41. DIVISION OF THE ASSEMBLY

## Purpose

The purpose of a request or demand for a division of the assembly is to secure an accurate vote or to verify a voice vote by requiring the voters to rise and, if necessary, to be counted.

## Form

> PROPOSER [immediately after the vote is announced and without waiting for recognition]: "I call for a division."
>
> *or*
>
> "Division!"
>
> CHAIRMAN "A division has been called for. Those in favor of the motion that [stating motion just voted upon], please rise. The secretary will please count. . . . Be seated. Those opposed, please rise. . . . Be seated. The affirmative vote is 62; the negative is 47. Therefore the motion is carried."

## Explanation

A call for a division is in effect a demand that a voice vote be verified by a rising vote.

Any member, without waiting for recognition, may call for a division at any time after the question has been put to vote and even after the vote has been announced and another has the floor but before any other motion has been made.[1]

When a division is called for, the presiding officer immediately asks those members who are in favor of the motion just voted upon to rise, and after they are seated, he asks those who are opposed to the motion to rise. It is not required that those rising be counted unless a count is required by the rules or unless it is necessary to determine the prevailing side.

Any member has a right to insist on verification of a vote which he feels may not be a true expression of the will of the assembly, but he cannot use this privilege to obstruct business by calling for a division on a vote which leaves no room for doubt as to which side prevails.

The responsibility of announcing a vote rests upon the chairman. If he is in doubt as to the vote, he may verify the vote himself by taking a rising vote and, if necessary, by counting.

### Effect

The effect of a call for a division of the assembly is to require the presiding officer to take a rising vote on the motion just voted upon and to count the vote whenever there is any question as to the prevailing side.

### Rules Governing Division of the Assembly

1. Can interrupt a speaker because it requires immediate decision
2. Requires no second because it is not a motion but a demand
3. Is not debatable since it is a demand

4. Cannot be amended because it is a demand
5. Requires no vote because it is the exercise of a right given to members
6. Takes precedence as an incidental motion over all motions except privileged motions
7. Applies to no motions but only to voice votes
8. Can have no motions applied to it
9. Cannot be renewed because the demand must be made immediately following the vote

## Chapter 42. QUESTION OF PRIVILEGE

### Purpose

The purpose of a question of privilege is to enable a member to secure immediate action upon a matter that concerns the comfort, convenience, rights, or privileges of the organization or of another individual or of himself as a member of the organization.

### Form

1. *Question of Privilege*

    PROPOSER [without waiting for recognition]: "Mr. Chairman, I rise to a question of privilege."

    CHAIRMAN [without waiting for a second]: "State your question of privilege."

    PROPOSER: "I request that the north windows of the convention hall be closed, since it is very drafty here."

    CHAIRMAN: "Your privilege is granted. Will the ushers please close the north windows?"

2. *Motion Involving Question of Privilege*

    PROPOSER: "As a question of privilege I move that the sergeant at arms be directed to have a loud-speaker system installed in this auditorium as quickly as possible."

## Explanation

There are times when it is necessary for a member to exercise his right to request immediate decision by the presiding officer or by the assembly on questions which concern the convenience, comfort, or rights of the assembly or of another member or of himself.

The importance or emergency nature of the question of privilege allows the member proposing it to interrupt a speaker. When the request is made by rising to a question of privilege, the presiding officer should rule immediately upon the privilege by stating that it is granted or denied. Any member may appeal from this decision.

If the question of privilege has interrupted a speaker, the presiding officer may rule that it is a legitimate question of privilege but not of sufficient urgency to interrupt further. He then states that the privilege will be granted when the speaker has concluded.

If the presiding officer decides that the question of privilege is a legitimate privilege and of sufficient urgency, he grants the privilege and proceeds to carry out the request immediately. As soon as the question of privilege has been disposed of, the speaker who was interrupted again resumes the floor.

Questions of privilege which relate primarily to a member are known as questions of "personal privilege." Questions which relate to the privileges of the entire assembly are known as questions of "privilege of the assembly" and have precedence over questions of personal privilege. Questions of privilege may also be raised by motions.

## Questions of Personal Privilege

Questions of personal privilege are those which pertain to an individual member in relation to the assembly or its business and under which a member can request, but not demand, the granting of a privilege. An example of personal privilege is the right of a member to rise to a question of privilege if the minutes contain a statement concerning him which he considers untrue.

## Questions of Privilege of the Assembly

Examples of questions of privilege of the assembly which frequently arise are those relating to the heating, lighting, ventilation, the seating of members, the accuracy of reports or papers, the conduct of officers or members or employees, the control of noise or members walking about, the ability to hear speakers, or the functioning of the public address system.

## Motions as Questions of Privilege

Sometimes it is necessary to propose a motion which is of immediate urgency. This can be done by rising to a question of privilege and presenting the motion. For example, if during a convention the discussion on a motion proved to be of a nature that would be embarrassing if made public, yet the motion required immediate decision, the chairman might allow a member, as a question of privilege, to move that non-members be requested to leave for the remainder of the meeting.

## Effect

If a question of privilege interrupts a speaker, he should be seated until the question of privilege is decided. If the chairman decides that the question of privilege is a legitimate privilege and of sufficient urgency, he grants the privilege and proceeds to carry out the request immediately.

As soon as the question of privilege has been disposed of, the speaker who was interrupted again resumes the floor.

*Rules Governing a Question of Privilege (Not a Motion)*

1. Can interrupt a speaker because it requires immediate action
2. Requires no second because it is a request and not a true motion
3. Is not debatable because it is decided by the presiding officer
4. Cannot be amended
5. Requires no vote because it is decided by the presiding officer
6. Takes precedence of all motions except the motions to adjourn and to recess
7. Applies to no other motion, since it is a request
8. Can have no other motions applied to it except withdraw
9. Cannot be renewed

When a question of privilege is presented as a motion, it is, after being stated by the chairman, subject to all the rules applicable to a main motion.

# Chapter 43. MOTION TO RECESS

## Purpose

The purpose of the motion to recess is to permit an interlude in a meeting.

## Form

PROPOSER: "I move that this assembly take a recess of five minutes."

*or*

"I move that we recess until tomorrow evening."

CHAIRMAN: "It has been moved and seconded that this assembly take a recess of five minutes. Those in favor say, 'Aye.' . . . Those opposed, 'No.' The motion is carried. The meeting is recessed for five minutes."

## Explanation

It may be necessary or convenient to recess while waiting for a speaker, while counting ballots, and in many other instances. A recess is an interval during a meeting, whereas an adjournment terminates a meeting. The motion to recess may be amended only as to the time or duration of the recess. It takes effect immediately unless the motion itself specifies to the contrary. A recess cannot extend beyond the time set for the next regular meeting.

The motion to "adjourn" to an adjourned meeting is, in effect, a motion to recess since an adjournment would terminate the meeting and an adjourned meeting is a continuation of a previous meeting.

Like all privileged motions, the motion to recess is a main motion if made when nothing else is before the assembly or when the recess is set for a future time. When made as a main motion, it follows all the rules of a main motion.

## Effect

The motion to take a recess suspends the meeting until the time stated for reconvening. When the assembly reconvenes, business is resumed at the point where it was interrupted.

## Rules Governing Motion to Recess

1. Cannot interrupt a speaker
2. Requires a second
3. Is not debatable
4. Can be amended only as to the time or duration of the recess, since it is otherwise invariable in form
5. Requires a majority vote
6. Takes precedence of all motions except the motion to adjourn
7. Applies to no other motion
8. Can have applied to it only the motion to amend and withdraw
9. Can be renewed after change in the parliamentary situation

# Chapter 44. MOTION TO ADJOURN

*Purpose*

The purpose of the motion to adjourn is to terminate formally a meeting, convention, or conference.

*Form*

1. *Unqualified Form*

   PROPOSER: "I move that we adjourn."

   CHAIRMAN: "It has been moved and seconded that we adjourn. Those in favor say, 'Aye.' . . . Those opposed, 'No.' The motion is carried. The meeting is adjourned."

2. *Qualified Form*

   a. *Future adjournment*

      "I move we adjourn in ten minutes."

      *or*

      "I move we adjourn at four o'clock."

   b. *Adjournment to adjourned meeting*

      "I move that this meeting adjourn to Friday a three o'clock."

   c. *Final adjournment*

      "I move that this convention now adjourn."

238

*or*

"I move that this convention adjourn *sine die*" (without day, *i.e.*, without appointing a day on which to reassemble).

## Explanation

1. *When a Motion to Adjourn Is in Order.* The motion to adojurn has the highest precedence of any motion. It may be proposed at any time except that it cannot interrupt a speaker or the taking of a vote. If the vote is by ballot, however, the assembly may adjourn while the ballots are being counted or before they are counted.

The courts have held that any number of members have the power to adjourn, even though they may not constitute a quorum.[1]

2. *Qualified and Unqualified Forms of the Motion.* There are two forms of the motion to adjourn. The unqualified form, which calls for immediate adjournment without reference to any future meeting, is a privileged motion with first rank in precedence. A qualified motion to adjourn is a main motion and subject to all the rules of a main motion; it is, therefore, debatable and may be amended and have any other motion applied to it. It is of lowest rank in precedence.

3. *When the Time for Adjournment Has Been Fixed.* When a definite hour for adjournment has been fixed by adoption of a program or by a rule or by a previous motion, it is the duty of the presiding officer, when that hour arrives, to interrupt a speaker or any pending business and call attention to the fact that it is time to adjourn. A member should then move to adjourn or to suspend the rule requiring adjournment. The latter motion requires a two-thirds vote.

The better form for such a rule would be to adjourn at a fixed time "unless otherwise ordered." When the time of adjournment is stated in this more flexible way, it can be changed by a majority vote.

4. *Motion to Adjourn to an Adjourned Meeting.* The motion to adjourn to an adjourned meeting is a qualified motion to adjourn and, therefore, subject to debate and amendment. No exact form is required but it is essential that it be clear that the meeting is to continue at a later date, and that the time and place of that continuation be stated. This is because no additional notice of the adjourned meeting is required unless specifically required in the rules.

The interval between the meeting which is adjourned and the adjourned meeting is, in fact, a recess, and the adjourned meeting is actually a part of the meeting which was adjourned.

5. *When Adjournment Would Dissolve.* There is one important exception to the rule that an unqualified motion to adjourn is a privileged motion. If an unqualified motion to adjourn is made when there is no provision in the constitution, bylaws, rules of order, or program for another meeting, the motion is, in fact, a motion to dissolve and is a main motion. The presiding officer should call the attention of the assembly to this situation; otherwise the assembly might be dissolved because it overlooked the fact that no time had been set for a further meeting. Such consequences warrant full discussion and opportunity to amend. Therefore, when there is no provision for a future meeting, even the unqualified motion to adjourn is in fact a motion to dissolve (a main motion) and is subject to all the rules of a main motion. This rule developed as a safeguard against inadvertent dissolution of an organization or of a convention.

One writer on parliamentary procedure listed a motion called "To fix the time to which to adjourn" and gave it the highest precedence in order to prevent inadvertent adjournments without provision for future meetings. He overlooked the fact that when there is no provision for other meetings, an unqualified motion to adjourn is, in fact, a motion to dissolve and as a main motion is subject to debate and amendment. The motion "To fix the time to which to adjourn" was copied from a special rule in Congress. It never became established in general usage and was soon discarded as a privileged motion, even in Congress, as being unnecessary and "because of the facility with which it was used in obstructive tactics." [2]

A final adjournment which has the effect of dissolving the assembly or closing the convention is termed "adjournment *sine die*," or adjournment without day.

6. *Completion of Business before Adjournment*. When any motion to adjourn is made, it is the duty of the presiding officer to see that no important business is overlooked before putting the motion to vote. Even though the unqualified motion to adjourn has been moved, the presiding officer may call the attention of the assembly to matters such as:

1. The lack of provision for the next meeting or the necessity of fixing the time at which to reconvene
2. Announcements
3. Any important business which must be decided before adjournment

When the chairman calls attention to the fact that there is something requiring action before adjournment, he usually asks the proposer of the motion to adjourn to withdraw his motion until the business has been completed.

7. *Voting on Adjournment*. There is frequently confusion in phrasing motions to adjourn. The presiding officer should be very careful to ascertain which type of adjournment the proposer of a motion to adjourn intends and then rephrase the motion if necessary to make it clear. For example, a

member may say, "I move that we adjourn until next Friday at three o'clock." If the next regular meeting is scheduled for that date and hour, the member is merely calling attention to the time of the next regular meeting and is not moving to adjourn to an adjourned meeting. The motion should be stated as: "It has been moved and seconded that we adjourn." In announcing the vote the chairman may add, "We now stand adjourned until our next regular meeting on Friday at three o'clock."

In putting any qualified motion to adjourn to vote, the chairman should state whether it fixes the hour for future adjournment, is an adjournment to an adjourned meeting (in which instance he should state this fact together with the time and place of reconvening), or whether the adjournment is *sine die* or in fact a dissolution.

It is good practice for the presiding officer, in declaring any meeting adjourned, to state the time and place for reconvening.

## Effect

The effect of the adoption of an unqualified motion to adjourn is to terminate the meeting or convention, upon announcement by the presiding officer.

The effect of adjournment upon unfinished business is as follows:

1. When a meeting is adjourned, the business which was interrupted by adjournment comes up first under "unfinished business" at the next meeting.
2. When the adjournment closes a series of meetings, such as a convention, the business which was interrupted is dropped but may be introduced as new business at a future meeting.
3. At an adjourned meeting business is taken up at the point at which it was interrupted.

## *Rules Governing Motion to Adjourn (Unqualified)*

1. Cannot interrupt a speaker because it does not require immediate attention
2. Requires a second
3. Is not debatable since it is a simple procedural motion and particularly because its high precedence is incompatible with debate
4. Cannot be amended because it is invariable in form
5. Requires a majority vote
6. Has the highest precedence of any motion
7. Applies to no other motion
8. Can have no other motion applied to it except withdraw
9. Can be renewed after a change in the parliamentary situation

The motion to adjourn when qualified, or when it is in effect a motion to dissolve, is a main motion and follows all of the rules of a main motion.

## DEFINITIONS OF PARLIAMENTARY TERMS

*Adhere*—When a motion is pending, and other motions, like the motion to amend, are applied to it, these motions are said to adhere to the original motion, and when this motion is postponed or referred to a committee, these adhering motions go with it.

*Adjourn*—To officially terminate a meeting.

*Adjourned Meeting*—A meeting which is a continuation of a regular or special meeting and which is legally a part of the same meeting.

*Adjourn Sine Die* (without day)—An adjournment which terminates a convention or conference.

*Adopt*—To approve, to give effect to.

*Adopt a Report*—The formal acceptance of a report. Adoption commits the organization to everything included in the report.

*Agenda*—The official list of business to be considered at a meeting or convention.

*Amend*—To change, by adding, deleting, or substituting words or provisions.

*Appeal*—An appeal from a decision of the presiding officer requires that the decision be referred to the assembly for its determination by a vote.

*Apply*—One motion is said to apply to another motion when it is used to alter or dispose of the first motion.

*Assembly*—A group of persons gathered together for deliberation, whether an organized body or not. Includes mass meetings as well as organized associations.

*Ballot*—A paper, or a mechanical device, by which votes are recorded. Used to ensure secrecy in voting.

*Bylaw*—A rule of an organization, ranking immediately below the constitution in authority and above the standing rules. May often include the usual provisions of a constitution.

*Chair*—The chairman or presiding officer.

*Change in parliamentary situation*—Used with reference to determining when a motion may be renewed. A change in the parliamentary situation means that motions have been proposed or disposed of, debate has proceeded, or other changes have occurred to create a new situation so that the assembly might reasonably take a different position on the question.

*Charter*—Grant of authority, usually from a state to a corporation, of its franchise and powers.

*Common Law*—Law developed by court decisions. Judge-made law.

*Consideration*—Formal discussion or debate by an organization.

*Constitution*—Statement of basic principles and structure of an organization. The highest authority created by the organization.

*Convene*—To formally open a meeting.

*Convention*—An assembly of persons who are usually representatives or delegates of units of the same organization, or of different organizations, and are gathered to hold a series of meetings.

*Demand*—The assertion of a parliamentary right.

*Dilatory*—Tending to delay or slow up. Deliberate use of procedure to hinder or prevent progress.

*Disposition of Motion*—To act upon a motion by voting upon, referring, postponing, or in some way removing a motion from the consideration of the assembly.

*Division of Assembly*—A vote taken by rising to verify a voice vote.

*Ex-officio*—To hold an office, or position, because of holding another office, as a president being ex officio a member of the executive committee.

*Expunge*—To delete a motion or resolution from the minutes.

*Floor*—When recognized formally by the chairman, one is said to have the "floor." He is the only person allowed to speak.

*General Consent*—An informal method of disposing of routine and generally favored proposals by assuming approval of a request for consent, unless objection is raised. Also called "unanimous consent."

*Germane*—Pertaining or relating directly to, having definite bearing upon. Applied to the relationship of amendments to motions.

*Immediately Pending Question*—When several questions are pending before the assembly, the one last proposed, which the assembly must decide first, is the immediately pending question.

*Incidental Motions*—Motions relating to questions which arise incidentally out of the business, or order or manner of considering the business, of an assembly.

*Incorporate*—To form a group of people into a legal entity recognized by law and with special rights, duties, functions, and liabilities distinct from its members.

*Informal Consideration*—A method of considering a question without observing all the rules governing formal debate.

*In Order*—Correct from a parliamentary standpoint at a given time.

*Invariable Form*—A motion is said to have an invariable form when it can be stated in only one way and when it is, therefore, not subject to change or amendment.

*Main Motion*—A motion presenting a subject to an assembly for discussion and decision.

*Majority Vote*—More than half of the total number legally voting, or if by ballot, more than half of the legal votes cast, unless otherwise defined.

*Meeting*—An assemblage of the members of an organization during which there is no separation of the members except for a recess. A meeting is terminated by an adjournment.

*Minority Vote*—Any number of votes which is less than half.

*Motion*—A proposal submitted to an assembly for its consideration and introduced by the words, "I move that. . . ."

*Nomination*—The formal proposal of a person as a candidate for an office.

*Order of Business*—The formal program or sequence of different items or classes of business arranged in the order in which they are to be considered by an assembly.

*Out of Order*—Not correct from a parliamentary standpoint at the particular time.

*Parliamentary Authority*—The manual or code adopted by an organization as its official parliamentary guide and which governs in all matters not covered in the constitution, bylaws, and rules of the organization.

*Pending Question*—A question, or motion, before the assembly which has not yet been voted upon.

*Plurality*—More votes than for any other candidate or measure but less than a majority.

*Point of Order*—An assertion amounting to a demand addressed to the presiding officer that a mistake should be corrected or a rule enforced.

*Preamble*—An introduction preceding a constitution or a resolution, stating its purpose or the reason for its proposal.

*Precedence*—The priority of proposal and consideration of one motion over another, as determined by the rules of parliamentary law.

*Privileged Motions*—Motions affecting the comfort or convenience of the assembly or one of its members, and having the highest order of precedence.

*Procedural Motion*—A motion which presents a question of procedure as distinguished from a substantive proposition.

*Progress in Debate*—A change in the situation so that the assembly might reasonably take a different position on the question. The adoption of a motion or the disposition of business almost always results in a change in the parliamentary situation and constitutes progress in debate.

*Proposition*—A proposal submitting a question of any kind for consideration and action. Includes motions, resolutions, reports, and other kinds of proposals.

*Proxy*—A signed statement transferring one's right to vote or to participate in a meeting to another person.

*Putting the Question*—Submitting a question to vote or taking a vote on a question.

*Question*—Any proposition submitted to an assembly for a decision.

*Quorum*—Number or proportion of persons which must be present at a meeting to enable the assembly to act legally on business.

*Recess*—An intermission in a meeting, usually brief, which does not terminate a meeting.

*Recognition*—The formal acknowledgment by the chairman indicating that a member has the right to speak.

*Renew a Motion*—To present the same motion a second or subsequent time.

*Resolution*—A formal proposal submitted in writing for action by an assembly.

*Restricted Debate*—Debate which is restricted to the propriety or advisability of the proposed motion in relation to the main motion and which does not open the latter to debate.

*Second*—An indication of approval of the consideration of a proposed motion.

*Seriatim*—Manner of considering by sections or paragraphs.

*Special Committee*—A committee appointed to accomplish a particular task and to submit a special report. It ceases to exist when its task is completed.

*Specific Main Motion*—A main motion which has a name, a specific form, and is subject to special rules, as opposed to a general main motion. Some specific main motions are rescind, reconsider, and resume consideration.

*Special Meeting*—A meeting called to consider certain specific business which must be set forth in the call.

*Special Statute*—A statute having a special reference to a particular subject and not general in its application.

*Statute*—A law made by a legislative body.

*Standing Committee*—A committee to handle all business on a certain subject which may be referred to it, and having a term of service corresponding to the term of office of the officers of the organization.

*Substantive Motion*—A motion which presents a concrete proposal of business, not a procedural motion.

*Tie Vote*—A vote in which the positive and negative are equal, as a 20 to 20 vote. A tie vote is not sufficient to take any action.

*Two-thirds Vote*—Two-thirds of all legal votes cast.

*Unanimous*—Without any dissenting vote. One adverse vote prevents unanimous approval.

*Unanimous Consent*—An informal method of disposing of routine and generally favored motions by assuming approval of a request for unanimous consent. Is defeated by one objection.

*Unfinished Business*—Any business deferred by a motion to postpone to a definite time, or any business which was incomplete when the previous meeting adjourned. Unfinished business has a preferred status at the following meeting.

*Viva Voce Vote*—A vote taken by calling for "ayes" and "noes" and judged by volume of voice response. Sometimes called "voice vote."

# FOOTNOTES

## Chapter 1

[1] *Terre Haute Gas Corp. v. Johnson* (1942) 221 Ind. 499; 45 N.E. (2d) 484.

## Chapter 3

[1] *Brown v. District of Columbia* (1888) 127 U.S. 579, 32 L. Ed. 262; *State v. Porter* (1888) 113 Ind. 79, 14 N.E. 883; *In re Gunn* (1893) 50 Kan. 155, 32 Pac. 948; *Ellsworth Woolen Mfg. Co. v. Faunce* (1887) 79 Me. 440, 10 Atl. 250; *Dingwall v. Common Council* (1890) 82 Mich. 568, 46 N.W. 938; *Boggess v. Buxton* (1910) 67 W. Va. 679, 69 S.E. 367.

[2] *Choate v. North Fork Highway Dist.* (1924) 39 Idaho 483, 228 Pac. 885; *City of Rolla v. Schuman* (1915) 189 Mo. App. 252, 175 S.W. 241; *Duniway v. Portland* (1905) 47 Ore. 103, 81 Pac. 945; *Daniels v. Bayless Stores* (1935) 46 Ariz. 442, 52 Pac. (2d) 475; *Hill v. Ponder* (1942) 221 N.C. 58, 19 S.E. (2d) 5.

[3] *People v. Wright* (1902) 30 Colo. 439, 71 Pac. 365; *State v. Porter* (1888) 113 Ind. 79, 14 N.E. 883; *Swan v. Indianola* (1909) 142 Iowa 731, 121 N.W. 547.

[4] *Seiler v. O'Maley* (1921) 190 Ky. 190, 227 S.W. 141.

[5] *Morrill v. Little Falls Mfg. Co.* (1893) 53 Minn. 371, 55 N.W. 547; *State v. Riechmann* (1911) 239 Mo. 81, 142 S.W. 304; *Kimball v. Marshall* (1863) 44 N.H. 465.

[6] *Fisher v. Harrisburg Gas Co.* (1857) 1 Pear. (Pa.) 118.

[7] *People v. Wright* (1902) 30 Colo. 439, 71 Pac. 365; *State v. Porter* (1888) 113 Ind. 79, 14 N.E. 883; *Swan v. Indianola* (1909) 142 Iowa 731, 121 N.W. 547.

[8] *State v. Paterson* (1871) 35 N.J.L. 190; *Gildersleeve v. Bd. of Education* (1860) 17 Abb. Pr. (N.Y.) 201.

[9] *Enright v. Heckscher* (1917) 240 Fed. 863, 153 C.C.A. 549; Burton *v. Lithic Mfg. Co.* (1914) 73 Ore. 605, 144 Pac. 1149; *Federal Life Ins. Co. v. Griffin* (1912) 173 Ill. App. 5.

[10] *Shugars v. Hamilton* (1906) 122 Ky. 606, 92 S.W. 564; *Dafoe v. Harshaw* (1886) 60 Mich. 200, 26 N.W. 879.

[11] *State v. Ellington* (1895) 117 N.C. 159, 23 S.E. 250, 53 Am. S.R. 580, 30 L.R.A. 532; *Christoffel v. United States* (1949) 338 U.S. 323; *United States v. Bryan* (1950) 339 U.S. 323.

[12] *Pollard v. Gregg* (1914) 77 N.H. 190, 90 Atl. 176; *Ralls v. Wyand* (1914) 40 Okla. 323, 138 Pac. 158.

## Chapter 4

[1] *City of Galveston v. Morton* (1883); 58 Texas 409.
[2] *Shoults v. Alderson* (1921) 55 Cal. App. 527, 203 Pac. 809.

## Chapter 7

[1] *Wood v. Town of Milton* (1908) 197 Mass. 531, 84 N.E. 332.
[2] *Hill v. Goodwin* (1876) 56 N.H. 441.

## Chapter 8

[1] *People v. American Inst.* (1873) 44 How. Pr. (N.Y.) 468.
[2] *Commonwealth v. Cullen* (1850) 13 Pa. State 132, 53 Am. Dec. 450.
[3] *Terre Haute Gas Corp. v. Johnson* (1943) 221 Ind. 499, 45 N.E. (2d) 484.

## Chapter 9

[1] *United States v. Ballin,* (1920) 144 U.S. 1; 12 Sup. Ct. 507; 36 Law Ed. 321.
[2] *Cascaden v. City of Waterloo* (1898) 106 Iowa 673, 77 N.W. 333.
[3] *State v. Bandel* (1906) 121 Mo. App. 516, 97 S.W. 222.
[4] *Martin v. Ballenger* (1938) 25 Cal. App. (2d) 435, 77 Pac. (2d) 888.
[5] *O'Neil v. O'Connell* (1945) 300 Ky. 707, 189 S.W. (2d) 965; *Frost v. Hoar* (1932) 85 N.H. 442, 160 Atl. 51.

[6] *Reeder v. Trotter* (1919) 142 Tenn. 37, 215 S.W. 400.

[7] *O'Neil v. O'Connell* (1945) 300 Ky. 707, 189 S.W. (2d) 965.

[8] *Hartford A & I Co. v. City of Sulphur* (1941) (CCA. 10th) 123 Fed. (2d) 566; *Caffey v. Veale* (1944) 193 Okla. 444, 145 Pa. (2d) 961.

[9] *Coles v. Williamsburgh* (1833) 10 Wend. (N.Y.) 659; *Oconto County v. Hall* (1879) 47 Wis. 208, 2 N.W. 291.

## Chapter 10

[1] *Landers v. Frank St. Methodist Church* (1889) 114 N.Y. 626, 21 N.E. 420.

[2] *State v. Ellington* (1895) 117 N.C. 159, 23 S.E. 250, 53 Am. S.R. 580, 30 L.R.A. 532.

[3] *Ibid.*

[4] *Att. Gen. v. Crocker* (1885) 138 Mass. 214.

[5] *Chariton v. Holliday* (1883) 60 Iowa 391, 14 N.W. 775.

[6] *Ibid.*

[7] *State v. Hutchins* (1891) 33 Nebr. 335, 50 N.W. 165.

## Chapter 11

[1] *Young v. Benevolent Assn.* (1911) 8 Ct. App. Orleans 146.

[2] *People v. Goodall* (1917) 203 Ill. App. 189.

[3] *Hornung v. State* (1888) 116 Ind. 458, 19 N.E. 151, 2 L.R.A. 510; *Lawrence v. Ingersoll* (1889) 88 Tenn. 52, 12 S.W. 422, 17 Am. St.R. 870, 6 L.R.A. 308.

## Chapter 12

[1] *People v. Albany, etc., R. Co.* (1869) 1 Lans. (N.Y.) 308, 55 Barb. 344.

## Chapter 13

[1] *Chastain v. Baxter* (1934) 139 Kan. 381, 31 Pac. (2d) 21; *Bentley v. Hurley* (1927) 211 Mo. App. 51, 299 S.W. 604; *Medlin v. Ebenezer Methodist Church* (1925) 132 S.C. 498, 129 S.E. 830.

[2] *Grand Intern. Brotherhood of Locomotive Engineers v. Green* (1923) 218 Ala. 496, 98 So. 569.

[3] *Jardine v. Superior Court Los Angeles Co.* (1931) 213 Cal. 301, 2 Pac. (2d) 756, appeal dismissed, 284 U.S., 592.

[4] *Bobe v. Lloyds* (1926) (C.C.A. 2d) 10 Fed. (2d) 730; Certificate denied, 270 U.S. 663.

[5] *U.S. Heater Co. v. Iron Moulders' Union* (1902) 129 Mich. 354, 88 N.W. 889.

[6] *Elliott v. Greer Presbyterian Church* (1936) 181 S.C. 84, 186 S.E. 651.

[7] *Brown v. Protestant Episcopal Church* (1925) 8 Fed. (2d) 149; *Idaho Apple Growers v. Brown* (1930) 50 Idaho 34, 293 Pac. 320; *Cahill v. Plumbers Gas, etc., Local* (1925) 238 Ill. App. 123, 315 Ill. 211, 146 N.E. 130; *Hanley v. American Railway Express Co.* (1923) 24 Mass. 248, 138 N.E. 323; *Mac Affer v. Boston & Maine R.R.* (1934) 273 N.Y.S. 679, 242 App. Div. 140; *Saxer v. Democratic County Comm.* (1936) 161 Misc. 35, 291 N.Y.S. 18.

[8] *Branagan v. Buckman* (1910) 122 N.Y.S. 610, 145 App. Div. 90.

[9] *Ibid.*

[10] *American Baseball Club v. Johnson* (1920) 179 N.Y.S. 498, 179 N.Y.S. 898, 190 App. Div. 932.

[11] *Ostrom v. Greene* (1900) 161 N.Y. 353, 55 N.E. 919; *Witherspoon v. State* (1925) 138 Miss. 310, 103 So. 134.

[12] *Landes v. State* (1903) 160 Ind. 479, 67 N.E. 189; *Witherspoon v. State* (1925) 138 Miss 310, 103 So. 134.

[13] *People v. American Institute* (1873) 44 Howard Pr. (N.Y.) 468.

[14] *Kerr v. Hicks* (1911) 154 N.C. 265, 70 S.E. 468.

[15] *Idaho Apple Growers' Assn. v. Brown* (1930) 50 Ida. 34, 293 Pac. 320; *Treas v. Price* (1930) 167 Miss. 121, 146 So. 630; *Normandey Cons. School v. Harral* (1926) 315 Mo. 602, 286 S.W. 86; *In re Howell's Estate* (1932) 260 N.Y.S. 598, 145 Misc. 557, Mod. 146 Misc. 169, 261 N.Y.S. 859; *Latrobe Hunting, etc., Club v. Decker* (1928) 12 Pa. D. & C. 63.

[16] *Hartman v. City of Pendleton* (1920) 96 Ore. 503, 186 Pac. 572.

[17] *Myrick v. Holmes* (1921) 151 Ga. 437, 107 S.E. 324; *Barnes v. Church* (1934) 118 Conn. 521, 173 Atl. 226.

[18] *Reding v. Anderson* (1887) 72 Iowa 498, 34 N.W. 300; *Chastain v. Baxter* (1934) 139 Kan. 381, 31 Pac. (2d) 21.

[19] *United Mine Workers v. Coronado Coal Co.* (1919 C.C.A. 8) 258 Fed. 829; *Inglis v. Millersburg Driving Assoc.* (1912) 169 Mich. 311, 136 N.W. 443; *Rourke v. Elk Drug Co.* (1902) 77 N.Y.S. 373, 75 App. Div. 145.

[20] *Edward Hines Yellow Pines Trustees v. State* (1922) 130 Miss. 398, 94 So. 231.

[21] *Brotherhood of Railway Trainmen v. Williams* (1925) 211 Ky. 638, 277 S.W. 500.

[22] *McFadden v. Murphy* (1889) 149 Mass. 341, 21 N.E. 868; *Ostrom v. Greene* (1900) 161 N.Y. 353, 55 N.E. 919; *Branagan v. Buckman* (1910) 122 N.Y.S. 610, 145 App. Div. 950, 130 N.Y.S. 1106.

[23] *First Russian National Organization v. Zuraw* (1915) 89 Conn. 616, 94 Atl. 976; *Balukonis v. Lithuanian Roman Catholic Benefit Society* (1930) 272 Mass. 366, 172 N.E. 505.

[24] *St. Mary's Benev. Assn. v. Lynch* (1887) 64 N.H. 213, 9 Atl. 98; *Industrial Trust Co. v. Greene* (1892) 17 R.I. 586, 23 Atl. 914.

[25] *Rosenthal v. Reinfeld* (1905) 96 N.Y.S. 199, 48 Misc. 652.

[26] *Crawford v. Athletic Assn.* (1900) 111 Iowa 736, 82 N.W. 944.

## Chapter 14

[1] *Witherspoon v. State* (1925) 138 Miss. 310, 103 So. 134.

[2] *Polin v. Kaplan* (1931) 257 N.Y. 277, 177 N.E. 833.

[3] *Gallaher v. American Legion* (1934) 154 Misc. 281, 277 N.Y.S. 81; *Oyster v. Slovene Nat. Ben. Society* (1935) 154 Misc. 19, 278 N.Y.S. 320.

[4] *Landes v. State* (1903) 160 Ind. 479, 67 N.E. 189.

## Chapter 19

[1] *Simons v. Berry* (1924) 205 N.Y.S. 442, 210 App. Div. 90.

[2] *Harris v. Thomas* (1920) (Tex. Civ. App.) 217 S.W. 1068.

[3] *Importers' and Exporters' Ins. Co. v. Rhoades* (1924) 205 N.Y.S. 628, 209 App. Div. 689.

[4] *Arnold v. Burgess* (1934) 272 N.Y.S. 534, 231 App. Div. 364.

[5] *Troy Iron and Nail Factory v. Corning* (1864) 45 Barb. (N.Y.) 231.

[6] *Austin v. Searing* (1857) 16 N.Y. 112, 69 Am. Dec. 665.

[7] *Brotherhood of Railroad Trainmen v. Williams* (1925) 211 Ky. 638, 277 S.W. 500; *Des Moines City Railway Co. v. Amalgamated Association of S & E Ry. Employees* (1927) 204 Iowa 1195, 213 N.W. 264.

[8] *Marshall v. Pilots' Assn.* (1902) 18 Pa. Sup. Ct. 644; *Hall v. Morrin* (1927) Mo. App. 293 S.W. 435.

[9] *Marshall v. Pilots' Assn.* (1902) 18 Pa. Sup. Ct. 644, but see (1903) 206 Pa. 182, 55 Atl. 916.

[10] *Hall v. Morrin* (1927) Mo. App. 293 S.W. 435; *Hillery v. Pedic Society of State of New York* (1919) 179 N.Y.S. 62. 189 App. Div. 766.

[11] *Elfer v. Marine Engineers' Beneficial Assn.* (1934) 179 La. 383, 154 So. 32; *Bersch v. Fire Underwriters Assn.* (1922) Mo. 241 S.W. 428; *Rogers v. Tangier Temple, etc.* (1924) 112 Neb. 166, 198 N.W. 873.

[12] *Jones v. State* (1890) 28 Neb. 495, 44 N.W. 658.

[13] *Otto v. Journeymen Tailors' Protective, etc., Union* (1888) 75 Cal. 308, 17 Pac. 217.

[14] *State v. Seattle Baseball Assn.* (1910) 61 Wash. 79, 111 Pac. 1055.

[15] *Polin v. Kaplan* (1931) 257 N.Y. 277, 177 N.E. 833; *Weiss v. Musical Mutual Protective Union* (1899) 189 Pa. 446, 42 Atl. 118.

[16] *Otto v. Journeyman Tailors' Protective & Benev. Union* (1888) 75 Cal. 308, 17 Pac. 217.

[17] *State v. Delaware Fire Company No. 3* (1922) 31 Del. 586, 117 Atl. 129.

[18] *Elfer v. Marine Engineers Beneficial Assn.* (1934) 179 La. 383, 154 So. 32.

[19] *Dingwall v. Amalgamated Assn. of Street R. Employees* (1906) 4 Cal. App. 565, 88 Pac. 597.

[20] *Evans v. Brown* (1919) 134 Md. 519, 107 Atl. 535; *Grassi Bros. v. O'Rourke* (1915) 89 Misc. 234, 153 N.Y.S. 493.

[21] *Shapiro v. Gehlman* (1935) 278 N.Y.S. 785, 244 App. Div. 238; *Bricklayers', Plasterers', Stonemasons' Union v. Bowen* (1920) 183 N.Y.S. 855.

[22] *Harris v. Aiken* (1907) 76 Kan. 516, 92 Pac. 537.

## Chapter 20

[1] *Haines v. Readfield* (1856) 41 Me. 246.

[2] *Tandy and Fairleigh Tobacco Co. v. Hopkinsville* (1917) 174 Ky. 189, 192 S.W. 46; *Coon Valley v. Spellum* (1926) 190 Wis. 140, 208 N.W. 916.

[3] *Hayden v. Noyes* (1824) 5 Conn. 391.

## Chapter 22

[1] *El Paso Gas Co. v. El Paso* (1899) 22 Tex. Civ. App. 309, 54 S.W. 798.

[2] *State v. Foster* (1823) 7 N.J.L. 101.

## Chapter 23

[1] *Brown v. Winterport* (1887) 79 Me. 305, 9 Atl. 844.

[2] *State ex rel. Burdick v. Tyrrell* (1914) 158 Wis. 425, 149 N.W. 280; *State v. Miller* (1900) 162 Oh. St. 436, 57 N.E. 227; *Regina v. Donoghue* (1858) 15 Up. Can. Q.B. 454.

[3] Cushing, Luther S. *"Lex Parliamentoria Americana.* Elements of the law and practice of Legislative Assemblies in the United States of America," Little, Brown & Company, Boston, 1856, Sec. 1266.

[4] *Crawford v. Gilchrist* (1912) 64 Fla. 41, 50 So. 963.

## Chapter 24

[1] *Schiefelin v. Hylan* (1919) 174 N.Y.S. 506; *Brown v. Winterport* (1887) 179 Me. 305, 9 Atl. 844.

[2] *Tetley v. Vancouver* (1897) 5 B.C. 276.

[3] *Naegely v. Saginaw* (1894) 101 Mich. 532, 60 N.W. 46; *Stockdale v. School District* (1881) 47 Mich. 226, 10 N.W. 349.

## Chapter 27

[1] *Wood v. Town of Milton* (1908) 197 Mass. 531, 84 N.E. 332.

## Chapter 28

[1] *Hood v. City of Wheeling* (1920) 85 W.Va. 578, 102 S.E. 259; *State v. Cox* (1920) 105 Neb. 175, 178 N.W. 913.

## Chapter 32

[1] *Terre Haute Gas Corporation v. Johnson* (1942) 221 Ind. 499, 45 N.E. (2d) 484; *Commonwealth v. Cullen* (1850) 13 Pa. 133, 53 Am. Dec. 450.

## Chapter 34

[1] *State v. Lashar* (1899) 171 Conn. 540, 42 Atl. 636; *Proctor Coal Co. v. Finley* (1895) 98 Ky. 405, 33 S.W. 188.

## Chapter 38

[1] *Rutherford v. City of Nashville* (1935) 168 Tenn. 499, 79 S.W. (2d) 581.

## Chapter 41

[1] *State v. Ellington* (1895) 117 N.C. 159, 23 S.E. 250, 53 Am. S.R. 580, 30 L.R.A. 532.

## Chapter 44

[1] *Choate v. North Fork Highway Dist.* (1924) 39 Ida. 483, 228 Pac. 885; *O'Neil v. Tyler* (1892) 3 N.D. 47, 53 N.W. 434.

[2] Rules, U.S. House of Representatives, Par. 784.

# INDEX